The Rise of Ecofascism

The Rise of Ecofascism

Climate Change and the Far Right

Sam Moore
Alex Roberts

polity

First published in 2022 by Polity Press

Polity Press
65 Bridge Street
Cambridge CB2 1UR, UK

Polity Press
101 Station Landing
Suite 300
Medford, MA 02155, USA

ISBN-13: 978-1-5095-4537-7
ISBN-13: 978-1-5095-4538-4 (pb)

A catalogue record for this book is available from the British Library.

Library of Congress Control Number: 2021941110

Typeset in 11 on 13pt Sabon
by Cheshire Typesetting Ltd, Cuddington, Cheshire
Printed and bound in Great Britain by CPI Group (UK) Ltd, Croydon

The publisher has used its best endeavours to ensure that the URLs for external websites referred to in this book are correct and active at the time of going to press. However, the publisher has no responsibility for the websites and can make no guarantee that a site will remain live or that the content is or will remain appropriate.

Every effort has been made to trace all copyright holders, but if any have been overlooked the publisher will be pleased to include any necessary credits in any subsequent reprint or edition.

For further information on Polity, visit our website:
politybooks.com

Contents

Acknowledgements

Happy acknowledgements pages are all alike; every unhappy acknowledgements page is unhappy in its own way. It is therefore a pleasure to report the perfect blandness of what follows.

We would like to thank our editor Dr George Owers and our three anonymous reviewers for their extremely helpful and generous feedback on the first draft of this book. We are indebted to Ian Tuttle for his speedy and exacting copy-editing, as we are to Julia Davies at Polity for her assistance throughout the process. We would also like to thank the rest of the team at Polity for putting together this book.

We would like to thank the guests who appeared on our podcast, 12 Rules for WHAT, during the writing of this book. Particular thanks, for their insights into the topics discussed here, are due to Andreas Malm, Lise Benoist, Samir Gandesha, Annie Kelly, Peter Staudenmaier, Joshua Citarella, Matthew Remski, David Renton, Mark Bray, Shane Burley, Blair Taylor, Jessica Thorne, Channel Rescue, James Poulter, Emerican Johnson, Spencer Sunshine, Alexandra Stern, Elif Sarican, Nik Matheou, Daniel Sonabend, as well as those many comrades who have elected to remain anonymous. We would also like to thank Adrienne Buller for her feedback on our conclusion.

I (Alex) would like to thank my family and Sam for his infinite patience in writing this book with me.

I (Sam) would like to thank Alex, Andrew and Cameron, my sharpest interlocutors. I would also like to thank my family for their emotional support during the writing of this book, their feedback on the manuscript, and for making me who I am in the first place, although I'm not sure anyone else thinks that was such a good idea. And to Amelia, thank you for everything.

Introduction

On 13 January 2020, we first put pen to paper for this book. Our argument felt clear and horrifying: as climate systems broke down, the centre of political normalcy would collapse, and people would find themselves looking for more drastic solutions. The escalating climate crisis would provide opportunities to all parts of the far right. Seductive neo-Malthusian arguments about overpopulation would bolster hardline security policies and borders, and give seemingly compelling justification for the radical deepening of racist politics in the Global North. The cultural tropes of uncleanliness, pollution and pestilence, which for centuries dictated the hierarchy of different people's places within, and access to, nature, would become more potent as people once again encountered the natural world as their antagonist. The interests of capital would swing behind authoritarian governments as a means to protect profits and growth. While we disagreed with some who had said that 'ecofascism' would be a direct and unavoidable consequence of climate breakdown, we thought such a project couldn't entirely be ruled out.

On the day we began to write, 41 people were in a serious condition in a hospital in Wuhan, China, their lungs

filled with a strange form of pneumonia, caused by a virus
which did not yet have a name. In a matter of months,
what came to be known as COVID-19 spread across the
world, and some of the social stressors we had envisaged
occurring with the onset of serious catastrophic climate
breakdown arrived a decade or three early.

Much of the response to the pandemic avoided talk
of the climate crisis directly. This is perhaps because the
diverse ecological problems facing us have sometimes been
simplified into the correlation of two measures: the parts
per million of atmospheric carbon dioxide and the rise in
global average temperatures. Such a simplification cannot
account for the increasing risk of pandemics, among a
host of other events. COVID-19 wasn't caused by a rise
in CO_2 levels, but it was arguably a product of the trans-
formative effects modern capitalist societies have had on
the environment.[1] It was perhaps the moment at which
we should have collectively and decisively moved in our
understanding – and not just in our terminology – from
'global warming' to 'climate systems breakdown'.

The pandemic provided a glimpse into possible *political*
responses to future climate breakdown. Past responses to
climate crises such as extreme weather events had been
shot through with environmental racism and state violence, but the scale of total social transformation implied
by the word 'fascism' would have been hyperbole. Long
imagined in disaster-movie style as a series of blazing
hot summers and polar bears adrift, all punctuated by
the occasional cataclysmic wave, it suddenly seemed to us
that climate systems breakdown might actually look much
more like the pandemic did: mass death events, sudden
stresses on global supply chains, abrupt and previously
unthinkable changes to everyday life, massive discrepancies
in vulnerability across class and racial groups, a generally
increased anxiety, racially displaced blame, the tightening
of surveillance regimes, a sudden return to governments
acting exclusively and aggressively in their national and
class interest, the mainstreaming of conspiracy culture,

talk of the end of globalization, a retreat to protectionism, unprecedented measures that suddenly seem entirely necessary, the sudden collapse of livelihoods for billions of the world's poor, and a deep economic shock worldwide.

This book is not about the coronavirus pandemic, and we should not expect the politics that emerges in response to major climate events in the future to resemble it exactly. Climate change contains other kinds of crises: extreme weather events, migration crises, chronic and acute food and water shortages, climate-related conflicts and the like. Each crisis will be encountered differently, each response will be, as the governance of crisis always is, complex and multifaceted, and often suddenly amplificatory of dormant social forms. It is in these unpredictable consequences of complex crises that the threat of the far right lies.

Mass far-right environmentalism will not be born from a vacuum. It would draw on the history of reactionary nature politics, which we call 'far-right ecologism'. In the first part of this book, we trace the history of these ideas and practices, from colonial nature management to the rise of scientific racism and eugenics to the 'green' aspects of Fascist Italy and Nazi Germany through to the postwar overpopulation discourse, currents of environmentalist misanthropy, and lastly the securitization of the environment itself. It is tempting to lump all historical manifestations of far-right environmentalism together. But this would be wrong. Although Umberto Eco noted that fascists are prone to understanding their own politics as a 'singular truth, endlessly reinterpreted',[2] we should resist this tendency. The history we cover is episodic and disparate, although consistent patterns do emerge. Time and again we see 'far-right ecologism' as animated by the profound tension between capitalism's expansionist dynamic, which often entails the destruction of parts of nature, and its continual production of social transformation. It is a history, therefore, not just of far-right ecologism's ideas but also of capitalism's nature–culture interface and its attendant crises.

And what this history shows is that far-right ecologism has been, by and large, intellectually parochial, concerned with nature in a curtailed and limited form. Its sense of nature has been flattened by fixation on particular species or a single place. If they have, like the environmentalist maxim, often 'acted local', they have rarely 'thought global'. Nevertheless, such intellectual parochialism should not be underestimated: it has been capable, at times, of genocide.

Now, the overarching form of environmental crisis is anthropogenic climate systems breakdown. Chapters 2–4 turn to the various far-right responses to this crisis. Climate systems breakdown is no local problem, nor can it be resolved by force. The consequences of failure cannot easily be made to affect a particular othered group. It will not be solved by anything the far right has historically proposed. But nor is it irrelevant to far-right politics. Far-right politics has, since its inception, been intimately involved in the defence of capitalism, and the most important cause of climate systems breakdown – the continued extraction and use of fossil fuels – is, in the words of Andreas Malm, 'not a sideshow to bourgeois democracy . . . it is the material form of contemporary capitalism'.[3] Climate systems breakdown puts the structure of capitalism at risk and thus also the social order that the far right is committed to defend.

Faced with a crisis of such magnitude, the far right has diversified its nature politics once again, splintering into parts more or less accepting of the problem, more or less mystified, more or less ambivalent about the possible end of industrial modernity. There is no single far-right nature politics at the moment. Just as they have been throughout history, different actors are divided up by different ways of looking at the problem, various conceptions of what is and is not included in 'nature', profound disagreements about what the problem *actually is*, massive discrepancies in tactics, and conflict about long-term solutions to climate breakdown.

We have grouped them here according to their present political form: first, far-right parties and other parts of an emerging 'environmental authoritarianism'; secondly, the younger far-right and fascist movements whose comparative agility, lack of interest in immediate electoral success and lack of connections to institutional power make them arguably more dangerous in the long term than the current electoral far right; and thirdly, the 'ecofascist' terrorists, the best known of whom carried out the Christchurch mosque attack, killing 51 Muslims. Each of these groupings has distinct aims, distinct political methods, their own internal tensions and, often, pronounced antagonisms with other parts of the far right. Just as in our previous book, *Post-Internet Far Right*, the far right is treated not as an aberrant force external to and preying on wider society, but as the most extreme part of a distribution, involved in a complicated dance with the rest of society.[4]

The effects of climate systems breakdown are already widespread. But like any exponential process without end, it is almost all in the future. It is to this future that the final chapter of the book turns. Here, we address what we call the 'ecofascist hypothesis': the widespread anxiety that our political future might be 'ecofascism'. How are we to make sense of such a prediction?

We start with the future emergence of reactionary movements. In particular, we argue, the long history of climate change denialism on the right is likely to have unexpected, complicated effects on their future nature politics. Large numbers of people committed to mainstream right politics, most substantially in the US, have been lied to by those who denied climate change. When they confront this – and perhaps more importantly discover that in many cases this suppression of the truth imperils everything that their politics works to hold together – they are likely to radicalize, although, like all radicalization, it will be unpredictable. It is unlikely, we think, to generate a flood of new converts to the left. Two reactions here combine to make a particularly potent mix: a revolt against those who have got us

into this mess *and simultaneously* an attempt to hold on
to what some people already have, either as individuals or,
more worryingly, as racial groups.

If it scales up beyond this movement stage to become a
form of government, this future 'ecofascism' will have to
address the more pronounced tension that has animated all
forms of far-right ecologism to date: the tension between
capitalism's endless economic expansion and the affirmation and protection of the 'natural order'. We outline
two possible futures. In each, the far right serves as the
(perhaps unruly) tool of a large fraction of capital. First,
fossil capital, which allows the far right to continue its
current broad commitments to climate change denial (we
call it 'Fossilized Reaction'). Secondly, it adheres to the
interests of the security state and authoritarian capitalist interests more generally (we call this possible future
'Batteries, Bombs and Borders'), which are involved in
the geopolitically fraught process of securing the resources
for a green energy transition and securing hegemony in
a renewed era of superpower competition. Complicating
both of these is the possible arrival of far-right groups of
'climate collapse cults'.

Let us be clear about our target. The vast majority of
current environmental movements and organizations are
not on the far right. Nor are the concerns of environmental movements in some way 'fascist' concerns. It is not
fascist to care about nature. Our conclusion turns to the
responses we can make to such far-right movements, and
about how we can act in ways impervious to far-right co-
optation. Environmental movements must be politicized
around issues of climate justice. Many, of course, already
are. Yet, as environmental movements grow in importance, and the climate crisis becomes ever urgent, such
movements will accumulate and jettison models of the
world with increasing rapidity. And therein lies the risk.
The political valence of environmentalism has changed
before in the past. In the past, it was just as much an
interest of the far right as of the left. It has the potential to

flip again. Whatever the future, declarations that climate disruption will 'push all utopian visions and ideological disputes into the background'[5] or that people will likely retreat into a form of disengaged hedonism are clearly wrong. Climate systems breakdown will only get *more* intensely politicized from here.

Few books on the environment model transformations in politics as drastic as those outlined here. There are exceptions, notably *Climate Leviathan*. In it, Geoff Mann and Joel Wainwright outline four hypothetical transformations of politics.[6] Most similar to our outline of future 'ecofascism' is their 'Climate Behemoth', in which reactionary political actors oppose the globalization of politics but keep capitalism. Many parts of our accounts are similar, although we split it into two distinct parts. The second of these parts even has some similarities with their 'Climate Leviathan', which seeks planetary capitalist government. In our speculations on the future, however, we emphasize the brutal and decidedly national character of the securitization of adaptation to climate systems breakdown, and the fraught aspects of a renewable energy transition. This is perhaps simply a matter of emphasis. We are also less optimistic than they are about the long-term prospects of what they call 'Climate Behemoth'. They believe that its contradictions will make it fall apart. We believe that it is possible, although not certain, that the far right can gain by its contradictions, and not simply disintegrate because of them.

Another book comparable to ours is the recent *White Skin, Black Fuel* by Andreas Malm and the Zetkin Collective.[7] It details the imbrication of its two titular parts: the white skins of fossil fuels' most important historical advocates and developers, and the black fuel itself. It is mostly, although not exclusively, focused on climate denialists, and the racial politics that informs it. It differs from our project in several respects. Firstly, we deal with a rather broader set of far-right actors, and therefore in less detail. Secondly, Malm and the Zetkin Collective focus on climate change and the responses to it. Of course, the emphasis is warranted: global temperature rise exacerbates all the other ecological problems. And, more than that, it poses existential risks to humanity as a whole. But this focus makes it more difficult to see what is specific about nature politics on the far right: its concern with particular places, with particular natural features, with food culture, with gender politics, with overpopulation, with energy security, with ideas of racial and ethnic identity and much more. Although a focus on each of these aspects might be read as a way of avoiding what is *really* essential in the politics of climate change, we think understanding these more diverse figurations of nature is essential to grasping contemporary far-right ecologism and predicting its future movements. The complex effects of future climate systems breakdown will mean that political actors will be able to contest what the *really significant* parts of it are. It is in this contestation that the far right's more diverse nature politics will become relevant.

Others have argued that it is essential to maintain a conception of climate systems breakdown beyond the radiative forcing effect of carbon dioxide in the atmosphere.[8] We agree. It is important for engaging the interrelated collection of problems that exist. But it is also politically essential: full decarbonization of the economy, absent adequate responses to the panoply of other ecological challenges, would not defuse the far right's ability to use their ideas of a 'crisis in nature' for political gain or entirely rule out the threat of what has been called 'ecofascism'.

But should we call it that?

On 'ecofascism'

'Ecofascism', as a term, has a rather complex history. Bernhard Forchtner, editor of *The Far Right and the Environment*, notes that 'ecofascism' is a much-contested term, not widely used in the academic literature. He characterizes it as a 'fringe phenomenon' that has little impact on the existing political landscape.[9] We largely agree. Why, then, is our book titled as it is? There are two reasons. First, we are writing in anticipation of politics to come as much as reflecting on the politics of today. Second, we accept the anxiety about the future that presently goes under the name of 'ecofascism' as valid, even if it is not the most precise or useful term.

Let us look at some of the uses to which the term has been put. First, 'ecofascism' has been used as a smear by right-wing opponents of environmentalism. Perhaps most illustrative is James Delingpole's *The Little Green Book of Eco-Fascism*, whose subtitle, 'The Left's Plan to Frighten Your Kids, Drive Up Energy Costs and Hike Your Taxes!' says enough about its politics. 'Fascism' here is the generic bogeyman of government action.[10] It goes without saying that we are not claiming any similarity between left-environmentalism and fascism. Similarly, in line with the overwhelming critical consensus, we identify 'fascism' as an ideology of the far right, not of the left. To borrow a line from Frank Uekötter, author of *The Green and the Brown: A History of Conservation in Nazi Germany*, 'If you came upon this book hoping to be told that today's environmentalists are actually Nazis in disguise, then I hope you paid for it before reaching this sentence.'[11]

A second use of 'ecofascism' has also been to criticize the Deep Ecology movement by proponents of 'social ecology', most significantly Murray Bookchin.[12] In the 1980s, Bookchin used the term to describe increasingly misanthropic tendencies within Deep Ecology, a strain of environmentalism that 'ascribed an equivalent value to human beings and nonhuman nature, and rejected the premise that people should occupy a privileged place in any moral reckoning'.[13] Bookchin was responding to Earth First! co-founder David Foreman's suggestion that US aid to Ethiopia during the famine was merely delaying the inevitable. Much better, he said, would be to 'let nature seek its own balance'.[14] Bookchin was also responding to an article from the pseudonymous 'Miss Ann Thropy', writing in the *Earth First! Journal* in support of the HIV virus. 'If radical environmentalists were to invent a disease to bring the human population back to ecological sanity', wrote the pseudonymous author, 'it would probably be something like AIDS'.[15]

This tendency still exists within environmentalism, or at least appears to. Recently, it was summed up neatly by a single image from the early COVID-19 pandemic: 'Corona is the cure, humans are the disease.' This last example, however, is more complex: soon after its propagation, it was found to be the output of a decentralized far-right propaganda group called the Hundred Handers, who were attempting to destabilize and mock environmentalist movements.[16] However, the most dangerous of all, Bookchin argued, were the new forms of 'Malthusianism' and overpopulation discourse. We discuss this tendency further in chapter 1.

Other people have also similarly been called 'ecofascists', perhaps most prominently some of the rioters at the storming of the US Capitol building on 6 January 2021.[17] Here, the term refers to what has been more aptly called 'conspirituality', a mixture of 'wellness' beliefs, conspiracy theorizing and appeals to the natural world.[18] We address this tendency further in chapter 3.

'Ecofascism' is also what the Christchurch mosque attacker called his ideology. He used it to justify murdering 51 Muslims. A few months later, the same justification was used in the killing of 23, largely Latino or Latina, people in El Paso. This book arrives in the long tail of these shootings and is in part an attempt to systematize and explore some of the complicated anxieties that emerged in the wake of these atrocities.[19]

So how do we define 'ecofascism'? We must first take a step back. What is 'fascism'? Our definition attempts to synthesize the insights of the literature, hewing closely to the mid-twentieth-century historical phenomenon rather than trying to extract a trans-historical ideal type.

Fascism is a political form that seeks to revolutionize and reharmonize the nation state through expelling a radically separate 'Other' by paramilitary means.[20] Because it seeks to legitimize itself through a self-declared intimate connection with a homogeneous 'people', it also requires a dense mass-associational society.[21] This allows it to circumvent liberal democratic forms of legitimacy. Because its notion of the homogeneous people is totalizing, it seeks to recruit all of life, both in the sense of 'private life' and the 'natural world', into its project and thus develops a voluminous and highly normative nature politics.[22] This vast nature politics is a consequence of the prior encroachment of capitalism into life, also in the senses of 'private life' and 'the natural world'. Thus, fascism is intensely interested in the interface between humans and the natural world, and the ordering of social relations according to nature's laws. However, because its account of capitalism is mystified and racialized, it does not consistently oppose capitalism's incursions into life, but ascribes different aspects of this incursion different racial characters. Drawing from nature the bleak lessons of scarcity, competition and dominance, it affirms the 'natural' character of racial struggle and the superiority of its own race within it.

The dominance of a few white nations globally in the time of fascism's appearance was a consequence of the globalized system of capitalism in its colonial form. Yet, at the same time, capitalist expansion destroyed the natural environment and destabilized social relations. One of the most pronounced tensions in fascist thought is, therefore, its ambivalence towards capitalism: it is the source of much that fascism finds appalling, and yet, as the real motor of the domination that fascism affirms, it cannot be entirely rejected. Fascism responds to this ambivalence with a normative racial vitalism: the dominance that capitalism affords is affirmed and naturalized while at the same time its destructiveness towards aspects of nature (and the social relations embedded in nature) is criticized. One effect of the colonial stage of capitalist development is affirmed, the other rejected. We will explore this contradictory response in greater depth in the following chapter.

Fascism in power made use of the authoritarian instruments that the state had accumulated during prior periods of crisis and colonial expansion.[23] In doing so, it favoured the interests of the ruling classes. However, it also used these instruments to express its nature politics and attempt to live out nature's diktats. The homogeneous notion of the people outlined above demands purification, both to destroy the organized working class and the nation's supposed racial enemies. In its movement, party and state forms, fascism therefore tended towards violence.

It thus has an ideological aspect, a set of political techniques, a dependency on particular historical conditions, and an implicit class aspect, which only partially subsumes its other aspects.[24] To restate: fascism is a political form that seeks to revolutionize and reharmonize the nation state through expelling a radically separate 'Other' by paramilitary means.

Ecofascism names one aspect of the wider fascist politics: that part which most emphatically tries to affirm its natural basis, whatever the contradictory results thereof. However, we don't think 'ecofascism' is useful for describing any present political actor, except a few on the margins. The main reason is simply the declining utility of the term 'fascism'. Each of the political forms mentioned in the definition of fascism above (independent mass associational forms, paramilitarism, state authoritarianism, racial politics) certainly exists in places around the globe at the moment, but in each instance, they are only partially coordinated. In many places, their interests are opposed. Of course, this need not be the case forever. The last chapter of this book is an exploration of ecofascism's potential re-emergence through the climate crisis, but perhaps the main purpose of the book as a whole is to convert popular worry about 'ecofascism' into more clear-eyed opposition to the forms of racialized power that are wielded over and through the environment, be they 'fascist' or not.

If most of what we discuss is not 'ecofascism', then what is it? Other terms have been suggested, such as Jonathan Olsen's 'right-wing ecology', which contains three parts: eco-naturalism (nature as the blueprint for social order), eco-organicism (nature and society viewed as an organism) and eco-authoritarianism (illiberal politics as the best solution to the environmental crises) as its foundational elements.[25] As others have argued, Olsen's focus on Germany makes it difficult for us to extrapolate this to other contexts.[26] 'Far-right ecologism' has also been used to suggest a link between the natural imaginary of the far right and its social imaginary.[27]

We also use 'far-right ecologism' in this book, although our definition is slightly different. As with our definition of 'ecofascism', we must take a step back and answer another question. What is politics? Politics is the struggle to produce or reproduce a set of social roles and relations. Our definition of 'far right' locates a particular position within this struggle. More a taxonomic family than a species, we define it as 'those forms of political behaviour which work on or advocate for the reproduction of capitalist social roles and relations on the basis of ethnic nationalism, racism, xenophobia or antisemitism, often through the application of violent means at odds with principles of formal equality and thus at least publicly unavailable to the liberal state'. Because of its generality, 'the far right' doesn't have one particular organizing form.

'Far-right ecologism' names all manner of highly variegated attempts to produce or reproduce racial hierarchies in and through natural systems. In what follows, we focus on the crises that allow social relations to nature to be reformed or reasserted. This focus on crisis and responses to crisis is deliberate: the manifold crises of climate systems breakdown are likely to define the future of nature politics, and as they do, we must be ready.

1

A history of far-right ecologism

'Always, somehow, some way, silently but clearly, I am given to understand that whiteness is the ownership of the earth forever and ever, Amen!' (W.E.B. Du Bois, 'The Souls of White Folk')[1]

Humans and environmental change

Humans have always been an environment-making species.[2] By 3,000 years ago, our impact was worldwide.[3] And, for almost as long as there have been environment-making practices, there have been environmental crises, of massively varying scope and form, from local deforestation to soil erosion and declining food availability to the interlocking global crises of today.

These crises have frequently contributed to transformations in the balance of political power. The end of the Roman Climatic Optimum seemingly intensified the Western Roman Empire's existent problems.[4] In Medieval Europe, climatic change underlay the malnutrition that made the Black Death such a devastating blow. In turn (in western Europe) the sudden drop in the labour supply as peasants died *en masse* made labour power more valuable. Peasants rushed to the towns, triggering an extended period of class struggle, and, ultimately, laying much of the groundwork for capitalism.

In the modern era, crises are inextricably bound up with the dynamics of capitalism. As Raj Patel and Jason Moore have theorized, capitalism relies on the continual cheapening of naturalized inputs.[5] This doesn't make capitalism's relation to nature one of pure destructiveness, but means it seeks to put nature to work for it, at an ever-accelerating rate. For this reason, it might be better to call our current era not the 'Anthropocene' (which defines this period of our planet's history in terms of effects caused by all humans, apparently without distinction), but the 'Capitalocene'.[6] It is not humanity in general that has caused our contemporary environmental crisis, but the specific economic system of capitalism.

As capitalism's demands on nature expand, tensions appear between those who want to conserve a given ecology and those who want to utilize it in different ways. Deciding *what constitutes a crisis* is therefore socially contested and the experience of it is differentiated by class, race and gender, as well as many other forms of social distinction. For some, a crisis might appear as social with environmental implications, for others as an ecological crisis which cascades into a crisis of governance, and for a few as a symbolic crisis whose solution requires the reimposition of a 'naturalized order'.

Some responses to crisis have utilized components of what would become far-right politics: asserting strict racial hierarchies of care for, access to, power over, or positions within nature. Often, these stratifications have served an economic role as well as a symbolic one, which forced the revaluing of parts of nature and groups of people. All too often, this means an aggressive cheapening, such as by the denigration of Black enslaved peoples' right to life and freedom, or the systematic devaluation of women's labour. These responses restore a 'natural order' and defend property ownership.

We name as 'far-right ecologism' those forces that seek to produce and enforce racial hierarchies *in and through* natural systems. It is not one singular project, but a diverse array of responses to crises.

Just as nature is put to work in the expansion of capitalism, so too are concepts of nature put to work in its justification, invoked flexibly in response to the imperatives of profit and governance. Some aspect of nature is proclaimed its fundamental law: the distinction between the ensouled and the automatic, nature's capacity to model ideal social relations, its scarcity, its givenness by God, its ability to select, its racial character, its tendency to degrade, its distinction with the realm of culture, its competitiveness, its production of hierarchies, its morality or conversely its amorality, its tendency towards balance, its obfuscation by modernity, its threateningness and so on. This aspect comes to stand in for the whole of nature: it becomes nature's 'eternal lesson'. Yet, when these concepts of nature come to be cashed out in practice, they are often scaled down to more mundane projects: the defence of charismatic megafauna, or particular trees, particular landscapes and so on.

In far-right ecologism, 'nature' mutates between a bottomless resource, an exotic threat, a final explanation, a weapon and a regulatory ideal. As a weapon, it is dangerous. As a regulatory ideal it is volatile, because two opposed conceptions of nature conflict in this idealization. On the one hand, 'nature' is the central regulatory ideal of society, whose ultimate triumph is guaranteed. On the other hand, the far right believes that nature has been obscured *in fact*. And the process of resolving this contradiction, of reaffirming 'nature', often involves the violence of nature's most ardent exemplars: a particular race.

How have ideas of nature been deployed historically to produce forms of racial domination? We proceed in roughly chronological order, outlining the major themes of successive periods: colonialism, fascism and the postwar period. We start with colonialism, not because it was identical with fascism but because it was a historical period and form of capitalism that laid the groundwork for the contemporary global distribution of power through a massive expansion in capitalism's ability to metabolize natural inputs and justified itself through racist ideas claiming some basis in nature.[7] Situating the contemporary far right in the long tail of colonialism allows us to stop imagining that all far-right politics is fascism while also letting us see how the death camps of Europe were only possible after their technological development in the colonies.

Colonial nature-management

Capitalism was not born in the cities, but the European countryside. It converted serfs to wage workers and expelled people from the land.[8] Sometimes, in enclosing land that had been held in common, ecological justifications were used. Temporary measures to combat soil erosion turned into permanent enclosures.[9] At the same time, the reach of capitalism was expanding around the globe, gathering more and more of the planet into itself, and putting nature to work.

From the beginning, colonial expansion faced an environmental critique. The land drying out as trees were felled was widely feared because it could cause famine. However, the mechanism was not well understood. Christopher Columbus warned against the deforestation of the newly discovered 'West Indies' because it might reduce rainfall.[10] Despite these fears, in practice, colonialism engendered widespread ecological destruction, an effect which stimulated the Western awareness of ecological change and necessitated rapid experimentation with conservation.[11] 'Climate change', after all, 'represented a major potential threat to colonial economic projects'.[12] Rather than preserving nature for its own sake, these early colonial efforts at conservation aimed at extending the lifetime of extraction. Soil erosion control, for example, was developed in the 'West Indies' during the seventeenth century, but the colonists were more concerned with the longevity of the plantation than the survival of the forest.[13] Such an indifference to nature for its own sake was not entirely shared amongst the colonists, however, and botany and other biological sciences flourished.[14] Scientists, plantation capitalists and imperial administrators each had distinct interests, a key source of friction in the early colonies.[15]

The colonists' economic concerns were supplemented by more metaphysical anxieties. While islands were often cast as 'Edenic', other landscapes were thought chaotic and hazardous. Environmental controls were imposed to bring them profitably back towards 'normalcy'.[16] Buffon proposed in the 1700s that climatic change would bring about the degeneration of crops and man alike: grander apocalyptic visions of the destruction of nature, man and his place within it (and it was *his* place that was imagined) were always looming behind environmental controls.[17]

If the environment had to be managed so strictly, what about the people? Perhaps the most important and influential pessimistic thinker of the colonial period was Thomas Malthus. In his 1798 *An Essay on the Principle of Population*, Malthus proposed that the fundamental scarcity of nature is in conflict with the sexual desires of an expanding population, a conflict 'fundamental to both morality and government'.[18] His pessimism was thorough: conditions of abundance, for instance, rather than bringing about higher living standards, would merely instigate further population growth, precipitating further disaster.

Malthus distinguished 'civilized' and 'savage' life. The former can exist sustainably and be granted freedom; the latter cannot control its consumption and therefore must be controlled. This profligate savage life was understood as indigenous, non-white and colonized.[19] Not content with having racialized the capacity for self-control, Malthus also claimed that civilized life was superior because of its unequal class structure, which 'checked' population: during famine the poorest would be unable to provide for themselves and so die off, whereas in an egalitarian society everyone would suffer.[20]

Malthus' ideas were used in colonial Ireland to argue against relief during the Great Famine (1845–52). Nassau Senior, a contemporary Oxford economist, opposed government famine relief on the grounds that the ultimate cause of the famine was overpopulation in the peasantry, beyond what the land could support. The only solution, which the famine brought, was sharp falls in both population and birth rates. Even this was apparently not enough. Senior was reported to have said to a colleague that one million dead in Ireland (out of a population of 8.5 million) 'would scarcely be enough to do much good'.[21]

Other critiques of colonial environmental destruction from inside the colonial system were based on medical concerns.[22] Climate became associated with the morally freighted notions of health and vigour. The terrifying disease ecologies into which Europeans had strayed were not, however, pre-social natural facts. Caribbean sugar plantations, for example, with their static basins of sugary water, provided the ideal setting for the spread of mosquitoes brought by colonists from Africa.[23] By the middle of the nineteenth century, European writing on the tropics had turned from its earlier celebration of the bounties available to fear of their nebulous pestilential quality, culminating in 'apocalyptic visions of the environmental harm caused by commercial exploitation'.[24] Even when, in the last years of the nineteenth century, parasitology superseded climate as the leading explanation for the effects of tropical diseases, the 'moral character' that disease conferred on colonial environments was preserved.

For thousands of years before the arrival of Europeans, Indigenous Americans used fire to produce diverse landscapes, in a huge variety of ways up and down the landmass. Nevertheless, when European colonists arrived, they declared the land 'pristine', and the Indigenous people were treated as mere extensions of nature – to be managed in the same way as the landscape. Australia was similarly declared *'terra nullius'* or 'nobody's land' because the Indigenous people had 'not yet mixed their labour with the earth in any permanent way'[25] – an idea with its origins in the thinking of English philosopher John Locke. On St Vincent, the seemingly innocuous project of forest conservation was used as a tool of political domination. As the island was mapped and planned out, the Carib population were excluded from consideration because their land use was thought 'improper'.[26] Robert DeCourcy Ward, coiner of the term 'ethnoclimatology', declared in the early twentieth century that in the tropics, 'voluntary progress toward a higher civilization is not reasonably to be expected'. Thus, the tropics 'must be developed under other auspices than their own'.[27] Conquest was justified by the apparent non-industriousness of the Indigenous peoples.

The opposite attitude was also used as a justification for appropriation by colonial states, a practice we might regard as an early instance of 'green-grabbing'.[28] Forest conservation under British rule in India[29] and French colonists' control of nature in Algeria[30] both emphasized the racial exclusivity of effective environmental governance. In the creation of US National Parks, Indigenous people were removed by the US Army for their use of a space that had been reserved for nature.[31] In colonialism's later stages, conservationism thus became a 'highly bureaucratized justification for state control of land use',[32] a tool used unabashedly to enforce existing relations of domination. The effects of such conservation 'were frequently just as destructive or oppressive in their effects on indigenous societies as direct destruction'.[33]

But does it make sense to speak of 'conservationism' at all in landscapes so totally transformed by conquest? The arrival of Europeans and their associated milieu of animals, plants and diseases transformed the environments of the Americas.[34] In the two centuries after Europeans arrived, millions of Indigenous people died through disease, slavery and war. Some have even argued that the immense environmental transformation this mass death caused marks the point of lowest atmospheric carbon dioxide, from which we are now rapidly accelerating away.[35] What was conserved by colonial states was not 'nature' in some pure sense, but nature already reorganized through the introduction of norms and species derived from European landscapes, and, most profoundly, 'organized' by the genocide of the land's previous inhabitants.

The initial infections in the Americas were accidental. But more deliberate forms of ecological destruction were also deployed. In the 1870s, the US army targeted the natural systems on which Indigenous people relied, most famously the bison, who were slaughtered to starve Indigenous Americans.[36] Once dominion had been secured, colonists worked to fix in place a particular ecology, 'destroying the natural tall grasses of the plains and planting short grasses for cattle', locking in both a particular form of land use and the particular set of social relations around it.[37] The arrival of the colonists, here as elsewhere, involved an ecological rift followed by an imposed stasis in nature use. Polemically, nature use in the colonies, even conservationist nature use, is an enforced peace after a triumphant war.

Towards Madison Grant

One of the key figures in early twentieth-century far-right ecologism was Madison Grant. He was influential on the development of more recognizably modern forms of conservationism, including the National Park system in the US (through his personal connections to President Theodore Roosevelt), the imposition of racist US immigration policy, the progress of American eugenics and the development of racialism. Most importantly of all, he was directly inspirational for Adolf Hitler. He cannot, however, be understood without grasping the variegated ideas he drew on, particularly the ideas of racialism and eugenics, nor can the bridge from him to fascism be understood without investigating the parallel, but distinct, development of the *völkisch* movement.

In racialist thought, 'Aryans' were at once biologized and sacralized. Joseph Arthur, Comte de Gobineau, 'the most influential academic racist of the nineteenth century',[38] declared in his 1853 *Essay on the Inequality of the Human Races* that all great human civilizations (Indian, Egyptian, Greek, Roman, German, Chinese) were the result of the ingenuity of 'Aryans'. 'Aryan', which had up until this point named a language group, was transformed into a biological race. It did not, however, correspond to common twenty-first-century ideas about racial groups. France, for example, was composed of several groups, which, conveniently for Gobineau, also mapped France's class structure. Regardless of the Aryans' astonishing purported achievements, he argued that degeneration was inevitable. Nothing could be done to forestall decline.[39]

In 1859 and 1871, Charles Darwin published the two most important books in the history of biology. It was in the wake of the intellectual crisis they triggered that Houston Stewart Chamberlain advanced racialism beyond Gobineau. Initially, Chamberlain employed a narrow and selective reading of Darwin to construct his theory of race, drawing parallels with selective breeding in animals. He claimed that Darwin's book was misnamed: it should have been called 'On The Origin of Races'. Ultimately, however, he came to reject the notion of natural selection and embrace racial categories with innate characteristics. The dominance of the race he called 'Teutons' could not, he thought, be based on a mere accident of natural selection.[40] Chamberlain's *The Foundation of the Nineteenth Century* summarized its titular century's racialism and anticipated the twentieth century's with its blend of mysticism, science and antisemitism (Jesus? Not a drop of Jewish blood, claimed Chamberlain). Nazi theorist Alfred Rosenberg claimed his *Myth of the Twentieth Century* as its sequel.

Chamberlain was responding to a different crisis in 'nature' than the earlier colonial administrators. Against an increasingly blurred distinction between humans and nature, as well as the increasingly widely accepted idea of universal equality, he asserted the superiority of a particular race. 'Nature' and 'race' became the all-encompassing explanations for the evident global domination of what we would now call 'white people'. 'Teutons' dominated because they were naturally given to it, and thus the mechanisms of their power required no further inquiry.

The characteristics that the racialists prized were fragile. The racialist Georges Vacher, Comte de Lapouge, emphasized in the early twentieth century that although the Aryans were unquestionably the best race, they were not the most 'fit'. They did not reproduce at the same rate as the lower races; thus they were doomed to be outbred. What had previously been held in check by Malthusian mechanisms no longer worked as the effects of famines were blunted by modernity.[41]

Similarly catastrophist, Gobineau had anticipated civilizational collapse in five stages as the Aryan race became more and more diluted.[42] Later biological discoveries seemed to give credence to this idea: August Weismann's 1892 discovery of the 'barrier' that bears his name seemed to imply that, because changes in the body during an organism's life do not affect the genes it passes on, all traits were strictly hereditary. Many desirable traits were thought recessive and therefore, once gone, lost forever. Thus, nothing could be done to prevent the collapse of civilization except control reproduction as tightly as possible.[43] A slew of American states passed 'one-drop' racial laws from 1910, which imagined whiteness as something that could be tarnished by even the slightest mixture.

If biology foretold doom for the white race, then so too did palaeontology. For centuries, fossilized creatures found in Europe were confidently expected to turn up as living creatures in parts of the world as yet unexplored: although individual creatures could die, the extinction of whole species was unthinkable. However, as it became obvious that these creatures would not be found, the idea of extinction was formed, first in 1813 by Georges Cuvier. Slowly, people began to worry about the extinction of entire human 'races'.[44] By the late nineteenth century, the extinction of the Indigenous peoples of Australia was regarded as a foregone conclusion.[45] Was it the Aryan's turn next?

And if so, what might be done in response to such a threat? Could the race be perfected and thus never go extinct? Francis Galton, polymath and public intellectual, expounded the first theory of 'eugenics'. He envisioned a system of state examinations and selective breeding to 'produce a highly gifted race of men' capable of managing the complex affairs of the British state.[46] His ideas reflected wider thought of the time: there existed desirable and undesirable traits within people, which were inherited rather than environmental; the principles of animal breeding were applicable to human reproduction; and contemporary societies had blunted the natural selection of superior traits within humans.[47] In eugenics, racial superiority is understood as based in nature, but requiring reinforcement beyond that which nature can provide.

Eugenics was extremely popular, and not confined to the far right. National Eugenics Societies popped up across the US and Europe, culminating in 1912 in the First International Eugenics Conference. In the 1930s, prominent American eugenicists were in dialogue with their Nazi counterparts, and hailed Nazi marriage and sterilization laws.[48] The influence went both ways: the Nazis' racial laws were in turn influenced by America's.[49]

Eugenics and racialism were reintegrated into nature conservationism by Madison Grant. A keen naturalist, it was on a trip to Europe that he noticed something that troubled him in the practice of trophy hunting for deer antlers. It wasn't – at first – the killing itself. Instead, Grant noticed that the deer killed centuries ago had larger antlers. Over time, trophy hunting for the largest antlers had left only those with smaller antlers to breed. Correlating the antler's breadth with their 'nobility', Grant deduced that hunting was causing 'deterioration'.[50] Ernst Haeckel had argued in 1870 that war was also degenerative, because the bravest men at the front died first. Slowly, Grant turned against hunting. An American patrician, it is important to note that Grant was writing as hunting was becoming industrialized; class hostility cannot be ruled out from this change of heart. Whatever the cause, he contributed to the shift from 'conservationism' (in which nature is left alone with the expectation of further exploitation later) to 'preservationism' (where nature is protected for its own sake).

The terror of 'deterioration' pervaded Grant's writing, along with the concept of the 'invasive species'.[51] But it was not just the deer that Grant thought were deteriorating, and not just animals and plants he thought invasive. He also campaigned fiercely – and successfully – for a halt to much of the Southern European migration into the US through the racial quotas of the 1924 Immigration Bill. Basing these quotas on the 1890 census, the number of immigrants, particularly Polish Jews, Greeks and Italians, was strictly limited. Asian immigration was effectively halted. These efforts he understood as forms of environmental protection.[52]

He was perhaps even more influential as a racial theorist. His 1915 *The Passing of the Great Race* is perhaps the most influential work in scientific racism. However, as his biographer Jonathan Spiro points out, 'almost nothing [in it] is original'. The book brought together common themes in wider racialist thought: race as a driving force of history, fear of racial extinction and 'race suicide', an obsession with purity, and the call for aristocrats to rule society.[53] His 1933 *The Conquest of a Continent* was less influential. An attempted last-hurrah in the face of the rising environmentalist anthropologists, who believed that the environment was more important to determine people's traits than genes, it was quickly forgotten. Nevertheless, it contained some of far-right ecologism's most characteristic configurations of racial relationships to nature. The Nordics' evolution in austere wintery climates over thousands of years had selected for good characteristics, Grant claimed, most importantly 'forward planning'. The trope was to resurface endlessly, from the mythic 'Thule' homeland of the Aryans to the climate-linked IQ differences of contemporary race science. It was also not original to Grant.

American Nordics like Grant were, however, no longer living in prehistoric Thule, but in New York. What special connection to American nature gave them the right to rule? Grant solved this problem by naturalizing conquest itself. The fact that American Nordics were not where their distant ancestors had been was explained by Grant as the necessary consequence of their deeper nature: their predilection for expansion and conquest. Non-nativeness, for the Nordics (and for the Nordics alone), became proof of their naturalized right to the land.

In a letter to Grant, Hitler described *The Passing of the Great Race* as his 'bible'. Grant cannot be straightforwardly described, however, as a 'fascist'. While he was undoubtedly a racist authoritarian who supported eugenics, his aristocratic attitudes kept his political machinations out of the street. Vacher had warned Grant that universal suffrage ensures only that 'power passes into degenerate hands', and Grant was likely to have agreed.[54] For fascism, by contrast, independent mass associationism is essential, as is the development of an all-important idea of the unified race. It is to the development of this idea that we now turn.

Casting their nets more widely than the more aristocratic racialists, *völkisch* political thinkers – starting a century before the arrival of Nazism – affirmed the intimacy of entire peoples (albeit still strictly constrained in their classes), or '*Völker*' with their lands, a natural condition imperilled by modernity. In the *völkisch* telling, certain environments were the forges of robust peoples, whilst others were detrimental. Their view of nature, although locally holistic, was highly particularized: 'Not all of nature ... but only its regional manifestations gave the *Volk* its character, potential, and unity.'[55]

Borrowing the terminology of Nordicism from Grant, Ludwig Ferdinand Clauss asserted that the German landscape produced a Nordic *Volk* that was measured and still. Even their language was determined by landscape. More profoundly still, the landscape seemed to give the *Volk* the deep capacity for intimate silence. In short, from the landscape came the possibility of spiritual community.[56] However, although this 'homeland' gained a kind of transcendental ideological status, what tied the people together was not just their culture but 'ties of blood': the *Volk* were a 'biological and racial community'.[57]

The *völkisch* movements were fearful of modernity; historian Peter Staudenmaier has called them a 'pathological response' to it.[58] They offered harmony in the rural landscape, a harmony that was social as well as natural: class conflict was to be ardently suppressed. We might even say that *völkisch* politics allowed 'nature' and a particular social system to be conflated. Class conflict was linked to modernity and urbanization: Wilhelm Heinrich Riehl claimed that the failed German Revolution of 1848 was caused by disorder springing from cities.[59] Other writers continued this anti-urban theme, warning that cities even 'threatened the reproductive capacity and vigor of the nation'.[60] Racial reproduction was folded back into ruralism. Cities were not just noisy and polluted: they were dysgenic.

And yet these movements were not entirely fixated on the past. They also pushed forward, tapping into the sense of an unfinished revolution which permeated German society from the late 1800s.[61] The contradiction between the desire for a 'revolution' and the need to suppress the revolutionary working class led to a concept of revolution that was strictly spiritual: a revolution to 'revitalize the nation without revolutionizing its structure'.[62] This did not mean it was to be a quietist or a private revolution. Instead, it found its scapegoat, and advocated, with increasing force, for its removal from society. The *Volk* was imperilled by modernity. And modernity, for many *völkisch* thinkers, was equated with Jews.

Fascism

Fascism allowed 'reactionaries' and 'modernists' to co-exist.[63] Because of this, it configured nature diversely, according to the particularities of its national variants. Some French fascist movements of the 1930s were decidedly rural. The Greenshirts arrived in a moment where 'both the government and the traditional farmers' organizations ... had been discredited by their utter helplessness in the collapse of farm prices'.[64] This collapse, which had triggered an agricultural depression across Europe, had been caused by the growth of the world food market. The increasing productivity of non-combatant countries during the First World War and faster shipping had depressed the prices that farmers could get for their food. Here cheap food – an essential part of capitalism's development – was the ruination of a specific class of food producers.[65]

It was in this context that the Greenshirts attempted to undercut strikes organized by farm workers and to restore power to the farm owners. They needn't have bothered: the state also organized to protect the harvest, prioritizing the needs of the city. Conservatives, for their part, decided that it would be more useful to simply influence the state with a lobby, and the Greenshirts were marginalized. They never managed to break through into being a catch-all party who could mobilize in both the countryside and the cities.[66]

A different dynamic played out between the urban and rural strands of far-right politics in Britain. Unlike France, Britain was heavily urbanized: the process had long since forced much of the peasant classes into the cities. Accordingly, Sir Oswald Mosley's British Union of Fascists (BUF) 'was overwhelmingly urban in character'.[67]

Nevertheless, the BUF had its nature ideologues. Jorian Jenks became an open member of the BUF in 1936. In

1937, he revised the party's agricultural policy, continuing his earlier advocacy for a system of family-owned farms (as he had in his 1935 *Farming and Money*). This rural revivalism posited a rejuvenation of rural life as a counterweight to the decadence and malaise of urban modernity. He combined it with the BUF's corporatism: an economic model based on a system of corporations that represented various sections of industry.[68] Jenks saw fascism as necessary to achieve his ecological vision. Its political methods were the only way he saw to overcome the 'money interests' (read 'Jews') he believed were set against rural reconstruction.[69]

Outside of the Mosleyite right, groups like English Mistery and English Array advocated for an anti-populist politics focused on the revival of a yeoman class and the rebuilding of an aristocracy committed to notions of service and responsible rule. Many of their ideas aligned with fascism, but they were averse to political struggle, an aversion which ultimately saved them from the internment camps of the Second World War.[70] In both the agricultural policy of Jorian Jenks and the writing of Rolf Gardiner (a member of both English Mistery and English Array, as well as a 'Nordic racialist, a pagan, and a keen supporter of Nazi rural policies'),[71] a connection was posited between a 'healthy' natural environment, including its food, and a racially homogeneous yeoman class.

Fantasies of rural idylls were less important for Italian Fascism, where the need to subdue and conquer not just other peoples but nature itself was a major ideological component.[72] Nature was not broadly the site, as it would be for the Nazis, of veneration, although Fascist Italy did establish National Parks early in its rule. Nevertheless, the same kinds of connections were made between land and people as elsewhere: the 'regeneration' of nature linked landscape and soul, but in this case not immutably. Instead, 'by changing the land, the regime aimed at regenerating the Italians'.[73]

Huge projects of reclamation and transformation of nature were launched, including dredging 75,000 hectares

of 'death-inducing' swamp. These marshes were considered 'sterile' and therefore had to be rendered productive.
Fuel and food self-sufficiency were the immediate aim, but
the project was also presented as constructing an 'ideal
landscape' in which the 'ideal Fascist man and woman'
could thrive. Militarism guided it: although entirely within
Italy, veterans' groups were sent to 'colonize' the reclaimed
land, and rural communities set up to support the project
were named after First World War battlefields.[74]

In Italy's invasion of Abyssinia (modern-day Ethiopia),
propaganda also presented nature as an adversary, to be
conquered as part of a 'benign colonialism'. War was
justified 'as a means to bring Fascist "civilization" and
order to a previously chaotic and underdeveloped African
"first nature"' and thus could be understood as 'a civilizing
and even humanitarian mission'.[75] Fascism and its wars
were worthy because they could subdue nature. Thus, as
Federico Caprotti and Maria Kaïka summarize, for Italian
Fascism, 'whilst nature as the ultimate nurturer of the ideal
fascist citizen provided inspiration for the regime's social
project, nature as wilderness posed a frontier that had to
be conquered and colonized'.[76]

How did the Nazis relate to nature? Some Nazis advocated extensive nature protection, but it was one idea in a
set of contradictory notions. Most importantly, there was
a profound tension (as well as a peculiar intertwinement)
between nature veneration and the drive to war. 'Nature'
itself was figured in contradictory ways: the tension between
a *völkisch* politics and modern agriculture; between a
metaphysical notion of race and its scientific delineation;
between the cultivation of life and its extermination: each
dynamic already traced here found its clearest expression
in Nazism. Its scale and the chaos of its rule allowed it to
express almost all the tendencies of far-right ecologism so
far discussed simultaneously, in their most complex and
intertwined forms.[77] Historian Charles E. Closmann summarizes that 'Nazi policies dealing with the environment
often demonstrated a combination of progressive measures

to protect natural resources, professional opportunism, and rhetorical appeals to national identity'.[78]

The flourishing of life for its own sake, far from being at the heart of the Nazi project, was eventually made subservient, as was everything else, to the strategy of rearmament: in 1933, production began on a massive order of 'agricultural tractors'. Ordered under the ban on rearmament, in fact, they were tanks.[79] As the Second World War progressed, Nazism's militarism steadily side-lined its nature-protecting wing, and many of its ecological projects were suspended in a crackdown on Rudolf Hess's associates after his ill-fated flight to Britain in 1941.[80] No regime so bent on militarism – which required the rapid expansion of the economy – could have been 'green' in any conventional sense.

Nor was Nazism in its environmental policies as radical as it wanted to be seen. German conservationists had long desired a national nature protection law. In 1935, shortly after the Nazis came to power, they got one.[81] Key passages of this law drew upon ideas and legislation dating in some cases back to the nineteenth century. Joachim Radkau summarizes: 'When it came to actual practice in nature protection, the Nazi regime largely carried on traditions from the Weimar Republic.'[82] However, in crucial ways they did differ from other conservationists, whose initial enthusiasm waned when, instead of the 'top-down approach to landscape preservation' they had wanted, they found themselves confronted by 'a command-and-control approach to natural resource exploitation'.[83] Nature conservation was subsumed by other imperatives.

There were exceptions to this rule. Section 5 of the law, for example, granted protection to 'other portions of free nature' which 'contribute to the ornamentation and liveliness of the form of the landscape or the animal world'.[84] In the famously scenic *Autobahn* project, the demands of rapid construction were held in tension with those of the 'Advocates for the Landscape', chief among them Alwin Seifert. Fritz Todt, who oversaw the project, intervened on behalf of these advocates, threatening to cut local builders out if the road was not sufficiently sensitive to nature.[85] These advocates also ran agricultural projects across Germany and occupied Europe, where they championed 'active engagement with shaping the German landscape'[86] through biodynamic agriculture, which combined a holistic view of farming with astrological and spiritual principles, understood as 'spiritually aware peasant wisdom'.[87]

Nature appreciation also played a major ideological role, just as it had in the popular organizations that acted as tributaries of Nazism. Even here, race ruled as an idea. Walter Schoenichen, who organized the *Naturschutz* (nature protection) movement, thought that 'between Aryans and non-Aryans there exist fundamental, unbridgeable differences, as for example especially in the areas of worldviews, sexuality, the relationship to nature, etc.'.[88] The Hitler Youth were called upon to 'take part in festivals that remind them of the inner connection between the landscape and customs of the various German tribes'. But war was not so far away: the ultimate goal of such connection was to instil the idea of the 'highest goal and highest task of all being solely in this: to be allowed to live and die for Germany'.[89]

What was the connection between holism and war? The sociologist Michael Mann highlights the transcendence Nazism strove for: suspending class conflict for the unity of race.[90] Timothy D. Snyder, by contrast, emphasizes that conflict and struggle were central to Hitler's worldview.[91] 'The Jew', Snyder argues, was for Hitler the symbol of false reconciliation between races. But the races could never be reconciled. Natural scarcity and consequent competition would not let it be. These two notions – transcendence and conflict – are not opposed. Instead, the only valid conflict was that between races, conceived of as distinct wholes, complete with their own landscapes, food, cultures and so on. Such a 'racialized holism' – we might suggest this is already a contradiction in terms – tended in Nazism towards Manichaeism: the absolute denigration of one racialized part of nature and the absolute affirmation of another.

This mode of thinking, with its underlying insistence on the fact of scarcity, could not, however, escape its own arbitrariness and historical contingency. Hitler's ideology was 'vulnerable to the simplest of pluralisms': that the earth could change. And the earth was changing. The Haber-Bosch process for fixing nitrogen, discovered in 1909 and industrialized a year later, was radically improving the yields of farms (and, in the First World War, allowing Germany to produce explosives). However, because Hitler thought scarcity was a fact of existence, it could not be undone. It was on this basis, Snyder claims, that Hitler was to refuse the reality of what was happening before him: massive increases in the productivity of agriculture that could have put an end to absolute scarcity.[92]

Why might Hitler have believed so emphatically in scarcity? Aside from ideological stubbornness, part of the answer might be the food shortages of the First World War. And the end of the war did not end the problems. The hyperinflation of 1923 distorted food prices and made it impossible to import food from abroad.[93] Further, the crisis wrecked the social structure of the countryside. Some peasants and smaller farmers bought equipment with loans, expecting hyperinflation would make their repayments trivial, only to become indebted once the hyperinflation ended.[94] Just a few years later, the second major economic crisis of the Weimar period triggered anti-semitic food riots. In 1928, Hitler, sensing an opportunity, 'clarified' the Nazi's policy on the 'expropriation of land for communal purposes without compensation'. It was, he said, exclusively aimed at Jewish speculators.[95] The complex tangle of biochemical, geopolitical, logistical and economic changes in food production that had struck the countryside were flattened into antisemitism.

In power, Nazis such as Richard Walter Darré – popularizer of the 'blood and soil' slogan – responded to these crises by affirming the 'peasantry' as the fundamental class of the German nation. However, reconstruction was not so simple. Darré's Reich Food Estate intended to harmonize the tensions in food production, but was caught in complex economic pressures, and the demands of cheap food for rapid rearmament crushed the peasant farmers. Soon Darré was considered a dreamer and his influence waned. However, his ideas were not simply betrayed as some have claimed.[96] On the contrary, Darré's ideology, in which Germany needed to expand into Eastern Europe to meet its food needs, 'provided the theoretical rationale for a program that aimed at the racial "renewal" of the German people, the elimination of Jews, and the conquest of *Lebensraum* (living space)'.[97] It is in the figure of Darré that not only the contradictions but also the overlap between militarism and the Nazi's nature politics became most striking.

In conquered Eastern Europe, Landscape Advocate Alwin Seifert declared that it was 'not enough just to cleanse the towns of past Polish mismanagement and construct clean and pleasant villages. The entire landscape must be Germanized'.[98] This 'Germanization' operated 'through murder, expulsion, expropriation, and other forms of ethnic cleansing'.[99] Werner Bauch, one of Seifert's corps of 'landscape advocates', was employed at Auschwitz, where he experimented with composting and constructed a tree nursery. Seifert directed the construction of a 180-acre biodynamic plantation at Dachau which grew medicinal herbs and other products for the SS. Countless prisoners died in its construction.[100]

During the war, scarcity had ideological utility: it was used to justify mass murder of people the Nazis considered 'life unworthy of living'. Public health initiatives expanded into the enforcement of 'racial purity' through the sterilization and murder of the disabled (including children), the sick and the Nazi's 'racial enemies'.[101] In the exterminations of the Holocaust, far-right ecologism reached its most brutal core, transforming the lie of racialized sensitivity to nature into a programme of absolute domination and control.

For their part, survivors of the Holocaust sometimes found respite in the woods and marshes to which they fled.[102] Nature was not infinitely malleable.

Postwar movements

A 'tidal wave of colour', as Malcolm X put it, defined the decades that followed the Second World War. Movements for emancipation forced European nations to give up many of their colonies.[103] The French geographer Pierre Gourou consoled the empire's supporters that the colonial retreat was not his country's fault, but inherent in the tropics themselves: their ungovernability was a permanent rule of nature, not a sign of imperial failure.[104]

The 1950s was also the start of The Great Acceleration, a pronounced uptick in production and consumption which entailed the utilization of nature on an unprecedented industrial scale. Human relations with the planet entered an entirely different level, 'unique in the entire history of human existence on Earth'.[105] A cluster of events worldwide in the 1960s and 1970s signalled the emergence of self-conscious environmental movements, many of which were left-wing: the publication and reception of Rachel Carson's seminal *Silent Spring*, which warned of the dangers of pesticides; the anti-logging Chipko movement in India; the Blue Marble photo taken from Apollo 17; outcry over the use of Agent Orange in Vietnam; and the Sanrizuka Struggle against Narita Airport in Japan, among many others.[106]

Later, the left-wing politics of environmentalism in the US would be affirmed by the African American-led protests against the dumping of toxic waste in Warren County, North Carolina.[107] In this example, as well as many others, the environmental effects of industrial development were and are displaced onto racialized people, who are then

blamed for their environment's degradation.[108] These
movements demanded not simply that the waste be moved
elsewhere, but that it be dealt with more completely,
showing that 'justice', as Andreas Malm and the Zetkin
Collective have written, 'is not the negation but the *essence*
of sustainability'.[109]

Amid this broader rise in left-wing environmental
politics, strands of far-right ecologism persisted in a sub-
terranean fashion, tendencies as marginal as they were
diverse.

The British rural reconstructionists continued their
activism. Rolf Gardiner and Jorian Jenks were involved in
the 1946 founding of The Soil Association, through which
they promoted organic farming. Jenks was *de facto* editor of
its journal *Mother Earth*. He did not renounce his fascism.
Indeed, he also wrote the agricultural policy document of
Mosley's postwar Union Movement, although he did not
use the Association as a vehicle for far-right politics.[110]
Alwin Seifert, Nazi Landscape Advocate, played a key role
in the development of the Organic Farming movement like
other Landscape Advocates, where they largely replaced
their earlier rhetoric of 'technical development [with] an
ecological vocabulary'.[111] Fascism and National Socialism
were adapted for a new reality.

Quite another mode of adaptation came through Savitri
Devi, who transformed Nazism into a spiritualist practice,
integrating it with Hinduism and animal rights advocacy.[112] In her ideological system, which she regarded as
the proper National Socialist conception of nature and
spirituality, 'nature' is the absolute regulatory ideal, the
imprecise centrepiece of an esoteric thought that waits
quietly for the return of Hitler.

More conventional than Devi, the 'cluster of think tanks,
cultural institutes and journals'[113] that constitutes the
European New Right also developed the far-right ecologist
imaginary in two ways. First, through Alain de Benoist's conservative paganism,[114] highly sensitive to space, critical of
hubristic anthropocentrism[115] and xenophobically allergic

to foreign intruders.[116] Second, through Guillaume Faye's future-oriented catastrophism, which bewailed 'Muslim extremism, the ethnoreligious clash between North and South, and the worsening of uncontrolled pollution'. Faye calls in response for a paganist society headed by a 'born chief' and the 'quelling of liberal democracy'.[117] These ideas the European New Right spread through a strategy of 'metapolitics', which dictates in its simplest formulation that 'politics is downstream of culture'. Metapolitics advocates for adherents to transform cultural institutions and in doing so 'conserve the fascist vision in the interregnum'.[118]

European far-right parties associated with the fascist past like the UK National Front and the German National Democratic Party attempted to use similar 'metapolitical' strategies, adopting environmentalism and criticizing existing green parties for not discussing causes like the 'endangerment of white Britons'[119] and the threat that abortion posed to the 'biological existence' of the German people as ecological concerns.[120] Their ecologism was almost exclusively understood through the frame of race, but their front groups were under-resourced; they gained little electorally.

Far-right ecologism in the US

The Soil Association, Savitri Devi, the European New Right, the various attempts of far-right parties to use environmentalism as a lure: if these moments seem peripheral to the major currents of postwar history, that is because they were. But in the 1960s and 1970s, environmentalism had become such a widespread discourse that actors across the political spectrum took positions in favour of environmental protection. Indeed, many of the strongest environmental protection laws in the US were passed under President Richard Nixon, no leftist. In America, other groups and thinkers on the far right mobilized a set of political tactics and aesthetics unencumbered by the fascist past, and would thus be more successful than the Europeans.[121] These thinkers also encountered the ongoing shift in the scale of environmental politics from particular landscapes to the entirety of the globe. In the 1970s, climate change was already known to be caused by rising CO_2 emissions.[122] These far-right ecologists responded to this and many other crises in ways variously catastrophist and denialist.

In the 1960s, Malthusianism was revived, most significantly by Paul Ehrlich's 1968 *The Population Bomb*. Predicting catastrophe, Ehrlich claimed hundreds of millions would soon die of hunger largely due to overpopulation. To solve such immanent and dire problems, neo-Malthusians flirted with compulsory sterilization programmes. The racial character of Ehrlich's predictions is unmistakable: it illustrated overpopulation as a Delhi slum seen through a taxi window.[123]

Ehrlich's claims did not come true. Over the long term, as it had been before, scarcity was becoming undone in important ways: the Green Revolution and the development of China, although they both had consequences too complicated to summarize here, contributed to cereal production massively outstripping population growth in the second half of the twentieth century.[124] Neo-Malthusian arguments frequently ignore that rarely is famine a consequence of there *not being* enough to eat, but is instead a problem of particular people *not having* enough to eat: a problem with dense layers of social mediation, rather than a simple natural fact. Gender and the politics of reproduction are also important dimensions of neo-Malthusian discourse. In *Reproduction Rights and Wrongs*, Betsy Hartmann argues that overpopulation became a driver for technocratic top-down population control initiatives, initiated by development and aid agencies and imposed on women in the Global South.[125]

In the same year as Ehrlich's book, Garrett Hardin supplied an ecological justification for privatization of the commons in his essay *The Tragedy of the Commons*, arguing that rational human self-interest meant that a collectively owned resource would, in time, be used to the point of depletion.[126] Hardin's argument that the depletion was unavoidable was wrong: the economist Elinor Ostrom developed practical algorithms for shared use of a common resource in 1990.[127] It also substantially misrepresented thousands of years of effective sharing of common resources by local communities.

Hardin's work also supplied far-right ecologism with its most important metaphor concerning adaptation to climate change. In 1974, he suggested the earth was like an ocean, on which some (citizens of rich countries) floated in lifeboats while other (poor, non-white) people were left adrift. Space in the lifeboats, Hardin asserted, was limited. This called for a 'lifeboat ethics'. For the rich citizens to allow others onto the lifeboat was to doom everyone: 'Complete justice, complete catastrophe'.[128]

Similar calls for immigration restriction on the basis of environmental arguments is the chief output of the Federation for American Immigration Reform (FAIR) network, founded by John Tanton. Having previously been active in the mainstream environmental group the Sierra Club, where he chaired its National Population committee in the early 1970s, it was in 1979 that Tanton founded FAIR.[129] It has attempted to make opposition to immigration acceptable from a liberal environmental position: more people in the Global North means more consumption and more pollution. This argument is more useful than Ehrlich's: scrapping the fixation on overpopulation (Ehrlich's argument was more complex, but this is what has mostly been drawn from his work), it instead set anti-immigration as one part of a wider environmental strategy. However, in homogenizing national and racial groups, it missed the most important determinants of ecological impact, namely, wealth. Environmental destruction was and remains tied to class and not race.

Tanton's construction of nature through 'exclusionary notions of nationalism, race and culture', as John Hultgren has it, ties him to a miscellaneous crop of thinkers more fringe than him.[130] Finnish ecologist Kaarlo Pentti Linkola welcomed events like war and genocide. 'Who misses the twenty million executed by Stalin?', he asked rhetorically, 'Who misses Hitler's six million Jews?'[131] Linkola held democracy in scorn, considering it unable to carry out the drastic decrease in the human population he thought necessary. Instead, he envisioned a world government overseen by a group of enlightened 'mutant visionaries' who would save humanity from itself.[132]

Linkola was an extreme voice, but by no means a lone one. Other writers on the wilderness, such as the American Edward Abbey, wrote in support of apartheid South Africa[133] and against the immigration of 'hungry, ignorant, unskilled, culturally-morally-genetically impoverished people',[134] namely non-white migrants. It was arguments from the group around Abbey – in praise of HIV, against food aid to Ethiopia – which Murray Bookchin described as 'ecofascist'.

As Keith Woodhouse, historian of radical environmentalism, has shown, arguments advanced by Abbey and others about the damage that non-white immigrants would do to the environment were contradictory: on the one hand, white Americans were considered the only plausible protectors of the environment; on the other, 'more people in the United States meant more people living a profligate and costly American lifestyle'. These arguments framed white Americans as 'at once the scourge of the planet and the stewards of a fragile landscape'.[135] By obscuring the stark class differences in consumption amongst white Americans – and thus presenting them as both stewards and destroyers – these far-right ecologists displaced blame for ecological damage onto racialized others.

If blame for localized destruction could be racialized, such a move was more difficult on the increasingly global scale of environmental politics. Although the argument has been made (repeatedly), it is arguably more difficult to sustain the claim that simple population had led to the billions of tonnes of CO_2 in the atmosphere rather than evidently unequal production and consumption. Instead, denialism developed gradually. The 1983 Nierenberg report, published under the Reagan administration, accepted the science of climate change but argued humanity could adapt to its impact.[136] In 1988, one of the worst droughts in history hit the US. It seemed climate change might be happening soon after all. President George H.W. Bush declared that he would counter the 'greenhouse effect' with the 'White House effect', and bring the power of the presidency to bear on the problem.

However, in 1989, the George C. Marshall Institute – an important institution in Cold War anticommunism – published 'Global Warming: What does the science tell us?', which contended that it was the sun, and not human's CO_2 emissions, that was responsible for global warming.[137] Eventually, every aspect of the science became contested.[138] Climate scientist Michael Mann calls this 'the illusion of a debate', the function of which is to create space for fossil fuel extraction to continue with minimum disruption. Until the present day, the vast majority of those on the far right deny climate change to some extent, a panoply of lies we will detail in the next chapter.

This about-face from Nixon's environmental protections to the full-throated denialism of later Republicans should perhaps not be surprising. Action on climate change is not contiguous with environmental protection more broadly; it entails a radically different scale of response. Environmental protection laws like the Clean Air Act aimed to improve public health by reducing pollution. By contrast, the fight against climate change requires a global transformation in the basic material substrate of contemporary capitalism: its dependency on fossil fuels.[139] It is no surprise therefore that fossil fuel companies, most importantly ExxonMobil, funded much of the denialist network.

They received support also from the wider right wing of American politics, where religious faith and capitalist imperative combined in neoconservatism to justify the limitless exploitation of the earth. Genesis commands, in a much-quoted passage: 'Be fruitful, and multiply, and replenish the earth, and subdue it: and have dominion over the fish of the sea, and over the fowl of the air, and over every living thing that moveth upon the earth.'[140]

What is the relationship of denialism to far-right ecologism? We argue that it allows for a further racialization of environmental impacts. It allows the cataclysmic social effects of natural disasters in the Global South, exacerbated by climate change, to seem like the consequences of racialized ineptitude, and not the effects of unprecedented anthropogenic climate change. However, this denialism does not work on its own, but in tandem with another tendency, much more accepting of the relationship between social problems and ecological destruction, but which responds by securitizing the natural environment.

It is perhaps significant that denialism was peddled by Cold War institutions in the post-Cold War era, like the George C. Marshall Institute. This 'redeployment' of Cold War institutions towards climate systems breakdown also contributed to the emerging environmental securitization discourse. Over the course of the Cold War, weather and the biosphere had become a direct concern of the security state, a process that also stimulated massive developments in the Earth sciences. In doing so, however, the security state 'monopolized definitions of both threat and security',[141] a monopolization which 'blocked action on nonmilitarized planetary threats, and specifically on climate change'.[142] President George W. Bush encouraged Americans to think of Hurricane Katrina *as if* it had been a nuclear attack.[143] Thus climate change – when it was not being simply denied – was addressed by military planners and others within a paradigm which placed 'risk management ahead of measures to address the root causes of environmental insecurity'.[144] In short, militarized adaptation to the effects of climate change, and not the mitigation of its causes, became the overarching focus of the response.

The 1990s saw a surge in environmental conflict discourse.[145] An article entitled 'The Coming Anarchy' by Robert D. Kaplan, sensationalizing the work of academic Thomas Homer-Dixon, declared that the most prescient image of the post-Cold War world was the widening gyre of chaos supposedly emerging from West Africa.[146] President Bill Clinton reported himself 'gripped'. The cause of these threats? 'Nature unchecked'. 'Here, as elsewhere in Africa and the Third World', Kaplan reported, 'man is challenging nature far beyond its limits, and nature is now beginning to take its revenge'. In Guinea, Ghana, Sierra Leone and the Ivory Coast, 'the primary rainforest and the secondary bush is being destroyed at an alarming rate'. From this apparently inexplicable environmental destruction comes crime and war.

Kaplan witnessed convoys of trucks taking the felled trees to the port. Yet, the cause of this deforestation is left unexplained. There is no word of the economic imperatives for logging. Kaplan's article stylizes Black people as tragically and dangerously overdetermined by nature. Capitalism has a tendency to destroy its own ecological conditions of production and in doing so engenders both environmental disaster and economic crises.[147] Kaplan projects this tendency onto Black people. A contradiction within capitalism becomes a racial character. In truth, in the globalized market, no environment is constructed strictly endogenously.

But these racialized threats, for all their recollection of colonial fears of Africa, were also strangely convenient. Although the environment was 'part of a terrifying array of problems that will define a new threat to our security', it provided a previously absent focus for US foreign policy in the aftermath of the Cold War. As 'the national-security issue of the early twenty-first century', environmental security allowed for the reorientation of existent security systems towards control of the problems resulting from environmental destruction, which Roland Deibert has termed the 'post-Cold War military-environmental security complex'.[148]

In contemporary far-right nature politics, securitization and denialism combine. Denialism attempts to push through environmental limits, externalizing the risks onto others. Securitization turns this risk into profitable control. Rather than two separate tendencies, they are increasingly aligned as two facets of the governance of nature and society: one produces and displaces risk, the other capitalizes it.

Far-right ecologism: towards the present

If denial and securitization are the most characteristic ways of thinking about nature on the right today, where are we now with far-right ecologism? Throughout this history, far-right ecologism's signal moment has been the claim that the 'lessons of nature' are directly applicable to social relations. This also explains its ideological function in capitalism. The far right wishes to enjoy the spoils of capitalist expansion without the social transformations that such a process entails. Racial domination could not have been achieved on the scale it was during colonialism without industrial capitalism. However, capitalism also entails ever-escalating production and resource extraction, destroying aspects of the lifeworld the far right wants to root itself in. The rootedness of people in the West (and their attendant social forms) is undercut by the force (capitalism) that gives that rootedness its particular character of global supremacy. In this sense, far-right ecologism stems from a misapprehension of the contingency of white people's historical global dominance. Far-right ecologism wants to maintain that dominance while denying the mechanisms by which it has come to be. Because the far right largely avoids using 'capitalism' to explain historical white dominance, it is instead claimed as 'natural'. Far-right ecologism and its diverse ideas of 'nature' paper over the ideological contradiction in far-right thought between the fact of power and its mechanism.

And 'ecofascism'? We can identify examples within wider far-right ecologism: Alwin Seifert, Jorian Jenks and Richard Walter Darré. What do they have in common? First, and most importantly, they were all fascists: they attempted to mobilize the racialized masses in defence of a set of naturalized social relations, in a way that circumvented liberal democratic norms. However, this was not the predominant mode in which far-right ecologism worked. Most conspicuous in much of the postwar period (at least from the neoliberal revolution onwards) is the absence of political mobilized masses. This is no accident. It is a structural condition of much contemporary politics to which we will shortly turn.

What does far-right ecologism look like now? Can *it* be called ecofascist? And how does far-right ecologism interact with the dominant governing mode of contemporary capitalism, namely neoliberalism? These are the questions we will answer over the next three chapters.

2

The far right and nature now

The contemporary far right is not a unified political move-ment, but a collection of disparate and conflicting projects. Some grasp the most powerful offices in the world, others fester on online platforms, others organize street demon-strations, and some carry out mass murders. This fractured and fractious landscape of different political forms is not structured arbitrarily, nor can its splits be entirely explained by the far right's political ineptitude or their narrow focus on particular nation states.

Our earlier definition of fascism contains three political forms: an authoritarian state; a racial mass movement; and extrajudicial deadly violence. These parts still exist on the far right, but as three separate strands. The fact that they are – for the most part – not integrated is the product of pronounced ideological differences, but also of the govern-ance of capitalism in neoliberalism.

Interwar fascism integrated all three: it utilized para-militarism and its claim to immediate expression of the will of the people to challenge and then assume state power.[1] However, such an integration is no longer viable in much of the world. In Europe, where the state's monop-oly on violence has become almost total, paramilitarism has become essentially impossible.[2] Violence is instead treated as terroristic and aberrant. Despite this situation in Europe, varying degrees of integration are still possible outside it: militia movements in the US; unaccountable paramilitary police in many countries; and the semi-paramilitary Rashtriya Swayamsevak Sangh (RSS) in India. All these are forms in which this extrajudicially violent part is more ambiguously distinguished from the state.

What about the split between movements and governments? This split is more recent, a product of the conventionally enforced prohibition (also historically contingent, also geographically variable) on overt biological racism and to a lesser extent on right-wing anti-capitalism. Accelerating transformations of the public sphere through the internet also contribute: many recent far-right movements have simply circumvented the traditional far-right parties by organizing through the internet.[3] This is again not to say that they will remain independent. The paradigmatic case of their capture is QAnon, which transformed America's deep wells of anti-government conspiratorialism into an appendage of the governmental far right. Conversely, the alt-right remained largely unassimilated, the prohibition on overt biological racism and antisemitism having proved too strong.

And the split between movements and violence? Both changes in the command structure of far-right organizations[4] (no longer are they so hierarchical) and the more general construction of the 'terrorist' as the singular bearer of violence allows for the production of this split.

These processes have not just split them up, but transformed them. As Wendy Brown writes, 'white nationalist authoritarian political formations ... are contoured by more than three decades of neoliberal assaults on democracy, equality and society'.[5] This three-way split is the product of a particular history. Thus, it might change again in the future, a possibility we explore in the final chapter on the future.

We should not treat these splits as neutral or unproblematic. Useful for clarity, they nevertheless each obscure an underlying continuity. The split between the governmental and the movementist far right comes with the danger of presenting racism as dispositional and aberrant rather than structural or driven by material interests. The split between the governmental far right and terrorists in turn naturalizes state violence. The split between movements and terrorists allows violence to appear as diametrically opposed to the slow cultural work of metapolitics, where in truth the former emerges in 'stochastic' patterns traceable to the rise and fall of far-right movements, and the latter can occasionally benefit from the attention afforded by terrorist violence. We return to these dynamics in a later chapter.

How do these splits affect nature politics? Articulations of 'nature' on the far right now are multifaceted, chaotic even. They address a plethora of different scales. Sometimes, it can seem that the 'environment' is only specific 'national' landscapes. Sometimes, it seems that what is at stake is humans' entire relationship to 'nature' as a regulatory ideal. These transformations of scale can be dizzying as the 'lessons of nature' are extrapolated from one context to another, from pollution to immigration to littering to global climate systems breakdown.

What explains this variability? Most obviously the far right's own diversity. But also the fact that, for the most part, nature is a 'thin' ideological notion, requiring further elaboration to be rendered a substantial political idea.[6] It is a *way of articulating* usual far-right talking points rather than the core of the politics itself. Accordingly, 'nature' changes in response to the demands of political goals. Despite this instrumental subordination to the needs of the moment, ideas of nature are important, functioning as 'an area through which these actors have long reproduced their ideology'.[7]

What almost all of the articulations of nature on the far right share, if only incompletely, is an opposition to 'neoliberal nature'. What is it? Neoliberalism's transnational character at once turns nature into an abstract and strangely *placeless* commodity (which denationalizes it),[8] while reinforcing existing geopolitical disparities in risk. The trees planted to offset your flight emissions could be anywhere, but the short-term impact of climate change will mostly be in the Global South. In doing so, 'neoliberal nature' 'updates older nature/society and fact/value ... dichotomies into a "systems/context" dualism'.[9]

It is this older dichotomy of fact/value that the far right attempts to resuscitate, and to do so in ways that are racialized and nationalized. The far right responds to 'neoliberal nature' by reaffirming nature's national character. Nature has been stolen from the nation by something at the scale of the international, an idea that applies both in the case of Jair Bolsonaro's obstinate exploitation of the Amazon and in the contrasting case of Rassemblement National's affirmation of a particularly French way of living ecologically. The forms of nature that are nationalized can be hugely various: not just an energy resource ripe for exploitation, a delicate local food culture, or of a particular kind of landscape.[10] Any kind of nature will do.

In this affirmation of nature's national character, ideas from the history of far-right ecologism come rushing back in: the idea that some races are naturally sensitive to nature or naturally industrious, that races are determined by their landscapes, that nature is fundamentally scarce and so on.

However, contemporary far-right nature politics is not simply the atavist regurgitation of colonial nature politics in opposition to neoliberal nature. Like Brown, we might even read much of contemporary far-right nature politics as stemming from neoliberalism's atrophying of society.[11] The conceptual transformation of neoliberal nature is underwritten by political and economic processes: privatization, securitization and financialization. The latter two can work to capitalize on environmental crises and in doing so deploy a logic of 'containment', whose built-in failures precipitate further privatization.[12] If far-right nature politics is an attack on neoliberal nature, it is one which maintains many of the underlying structures of neo-liberalism more generally, namely its moralization (as a replacement for social contestation), its marketization and its geographic and racialized displacements of risk.

If there is so much in common between the far right and neoliberalism, at the scale of both their general politics and their ideas of nature, in what sense do they oppose 'neoliberal nature'? Don't they just combine it with older notions?

To understand why it makes sense to frame much of the far right as opposed to what they understand as neoliberalism, we must turn to one of most startling but underappreciated aspects of contemporary far-right poli-tics: much of the far right thinks international capitalism and the left are the same thing. How is such a peculiar conflation possible? It rests on the central distinction of far-right politics: not between the dominant and the dis-possessed, still less between the international working class and capital, but between the national and international *per se*. Neoliberalism, understood from the far right as an international phenomenon (it is correct on at least this point), is opposed to the national, and thus is cast as 'left-wing'. This view is reinforced by the cosmetic support for social liberalism (and even some aspects of social justice) adopted by international companies, and by the seeming identity (although for different reasons) of left-wing and neoliberal support for migration.

This force (which they name 'globalism') is roughly what the left would call 'neoliberalism', although it also includes organizations like the World Health Organization and (importantly for us) treaties like the United Nations Framework Convention on Climate Change (UNFCCC). These it treats as if they are the seat of conspiracies against the nation.[13] It is true that neoliberal capitalism has atrophied the power of the nation state. But, in the con-temporary far right, international organizations feature more prominently in comparison to the (arguably more important) movement of global capital. In this sense, the far right understands that states have lost much of their power, but misses how.[14]

This focus on comparatively egalitarian international environmental organizations at the expense of attention to flows of capital leads to a situation in which Bernhard Forchtner can report that feelings of 'the neglect for "the little guy" by allegedly cosmopolitan, liberal elites' lead to climate change scepticism, a tendency itself 'embedded in a wider far-right imaginary which stresses the significance of local particularity in opposition to global abstractedness'.[15]

'Globalism' dissolves the power of the nation state and makes moral claims on it that it should not have to adhere to.[16] However, this is no clean break from neoliberalism (now viewed again from our own perspective). As Brown argues, neoliberalism's dismantling of the social makes claims to redress social wrongs outside of the market appear as special pleading.[17] It is this that fires up the refusal of social justice more generally in neoliberalism. When calls for justice come through international environmental organizations and treaties, the splenetic objections go into overdrive.

We can tie this back into the construction of 'neoliberal nature' more broadly: by addressing climate change through 'globalist' institutions, we might summarize, the far right believes that parts of nationalized nature are rendered equivalent and social justice, with its principles of equality, is advanced. A true – nationalist – view of 'nature' would obviate both.

The dominant currents of contemporary far-right ecologism thus work in a complex relationship to neoliberalism. They object to neoliberalism's tendency towards international cultural homogenization, understood as social liberalization and the redress of structural disparities, as well as to the homogenization of 'nature'. However, in response, they propose little else than the further radicalization of neoliberalization's underlying drive towards privatization, this time lodged firmly at the scale of the national. We might suggest, given the seeming irreversibility of capitalism's internationalization, that this is impossible. It is in facing this impossibility that the tendency towards violence might scale up.

This chapter deals with the contemporary governmental far right and environmental authoritarianism. In the same way that our history was structured in light of the present, this chapter implicitly looks to the future. The tendencies described here – the governmental far-right nature politics, the more general 'environmental authoritarianism' – are, at present, disconnected from each other. Both concern the governing of nature through authoritarian means, but in different ways. Nevertheless, their future integration remains possible.

Denialism

Denial has many forms: trend denialism ('the globe is not heating up'), attribution denialism ('it's not humans causing it'), impact denialism ('it won't have any serious effects'), action denialism ('we don't need to do anything') and urgency denialism ('we should act, but not yet'). Each one tends to forestall even posing the question of the next.

We might argue that denialism persists against the enormous weight of evidence because, as Andreas Malm and the Zetkin Collective have written, it accords 'with some pressing material interests of the dominant classes'.[18] This is certainly true. Denialism has historically been propagated through institutions funded directly by fossil fuel capital. And yet, there are other possible explanations. Matthew Lockwood has argued that the idea of a struggle between 'the people' and a cosmopolitan elite forms the backbone of climate change denialism rather than 'interest-based explanations'.[19] Because of fossil fuels' fundamentality to contemporary capitalism, however, we suggest it is difficult to isolate a distinct 'material interest' in continued fossil fuel extraction by anything as simple as checking a stock portfolio. We think both explanations are plausible.

In Germany as in Poland, domestic coal extraction has been vociferously defended by the far-right parties in opposition and in power (the Alternative für Deutschland (AfD) and Law and Justice (PiS), respectively). In Norway, a direct link between the country's welfare system (also supposedly threatened by Muslim immigration) and oil was made by the far-right Progress Party: without greater levels of resource extraction, Norway's famous welfare largess would be impossible, they declared, ignoring that neighbouring Sweden achieves the same with no oil reserves.[20]

President Donald Trump's climate denialism is well known. In 2010 he called climate change a 'con', seemingly citing the 'ClimateGate' scandal, during which denialists misrepresented errors in a climate change report to imply a conspiracy.[21] He has repeatedly claimed that climate change was a hoax by the Chinese. In office, his administration exited the Paris Climate Agreement, reflecting both the anti-international currents in far-right politics and wider concerns among Republicans that the deal made the US uncompetitive. His administration massively expanded offshore drilling and scrapped or weakened 112 different pieces of environmental legislation[22] including reducing vehicle emissions standards, a single change which would allow vehicles to emit a further billion tonnes of CO_2, or 20 per cent of the annual US total.[23]

Will this mode of climate denialism hold into the future? The interests at stake show no signs of abating, and they will likely have a willing avatar. Tucker Carlson, possible 2024 presidential candidate, has used arguments familiar from the Tanton network, explaining his hardline anti-immigration stance as a consequence of his love for the environment.[24] Carlson has vociferously denied anthropogenic climate change and rejected calls for climate justice, ridiculing them as 'systemic racism in the sky'.[25]

In Brazil, layers of historical domination coincide in the figure of Bolsonaro: colonial resource extraction, the denigration of Indigenous peoples, authoritarian neoliberal revolutions, Cold War anti-communism, reactionary sexism and racism, and anti-leftism. As Alex Hochuli has written, in Brazilian history, 'it is rare for matters to be definitively resolved . . . the new eventually vanquishes the old at the cost of incorporating the old into the new'.[26]

Bolsonaro's environmental impact has been devastating, not just for Brazil – but, given the Amazon's global importance as a sink of carbon dioxide – the entire world. The deforestation of the Brazilian Amazon was already on the rise before Bolsonaro, but under his government – elected in October 2018 – it exploded.[27] Between August 2018 and July 2019, it increased by 30 per cent compared with the year before.[28] The following year, a further 9.5 per cent.[29]

For all Bolsonaro's denialism, Brazil has some of the highest rates of concern about climate change in the world (a 2015 poll found some 86 per cent of the population thought it was a serious concern).[30] Against this overwhelming popular interest, the decimation of the Amazon stands out as a class project, lucrative for landowners and cattle farmers. It is perhaps then no surprise that Bolsonaro's Minister of the Economy, Paulo Guedes, is one of the original 'Chicago Boys', who have provided the ideological justification for the waves of authoritarian neoliberalization in South America since the early 1970s.

Despite this widespread public interest in environmentalism, the economy of Brazil remains focused on primary commodities, which must be sourced directly in the natural environment. The presidential terms of Luiz Inácio Lula da Silva (known as Lula) had been marked by the clash of 'environmental protection and social justice . . ., on one hand, and . . . the expansion of large-scale production systems on the other'.[31] As Brown argues, these zones of protection and justice are anathema to neoliberalism, which views claims for social justice as 'totalitarian'.[32] Such claims on social justice were perhaps rendered even more outrageous for the far-right/neoliberal alloy of Bolsonaro's base when the anti-corruption drive of Operation Car Wash seemed to reveal widespread corruption. It centred on the state-owned oil company Petrobras, on whose board both Lula and Dilma Rousseff, who succeeded him as president, sat. The scandal perhaps contributed to a situation in which Lula and Rousseff's records of social progressiveness (including their environmental policies) were read as hypocrisy.

Operation Car Wash has since been shown to have been systematically biased. Documents released in 2019 by The Intercept showed that the prosecutors had 'plotted to prevent the [Lula's] Workers' Party from winning the 2018 presidential election'.[33] But the damage had already been done: it undoubtedly laid the groundwork for Bolsonaro's triumph. Here, in this combination of anti-corruption drives, backroom dealing, and the rejection of all claims on social justice, the politics of the far right become most nakedly imbricated with the logic of neoliberalism: not opposed to it, but its flourishing.

In Brazil, environmental degradation comes with the degradation of Indigenous rights. The Bolsonaro government has made moves to legalize mining on Indigenous lands, obviously destructive to ecosystems upon which Indigenous peoples rely.[34] Two conflicting descriptions of Indigenous people by Bolsonaro bear discussion. On the one hand, he has presented them as allied with nebulous international organizations against the Brazilian people.[35] This description implies the nation (which apparently does not include its Indigenous population) is beset by nebulous outsiders, both inside and out. On the other hand, he has demanded assimilation through offering them the right to the privatized exploitation of their own land. Bolsonaro here makes neoliberal the colonial relationship in which humanization is predicated on religious conversion: privatized exploitation is at once a path to formal equality and catastrophic for the Indigenous people's relationship to the land.[36]

Bolsonaro's descriptions of nature were also directly redolent of colonial nature politics. His baffling declaration that the Amazon is 'practically untouched' defends a new regime of extraction by resuscitating the notion of nature as an inexhaustible bounty.[37] When denial is untenable – such as in the case of the enormous waves of fires of 2019 and 2020 – conspiracies are used instead. The fires, he said, had been started by those who wanted to 'make him look bad', echoing an American conspiracy that the California wildfires were started by the bogeyman of 'antifa'.[38]

The power of this absurd conspiratorialism – in which lying becomes so blatant that it functions as a demonstration of contempt for those who would hold the speaker to account – was perhaps even more developed in the case of Trump. Where Bolsonaro had conspiracies about NGOs and leftists, Trump had QAnon.

QAnon, and other mass conspiratorial movements, have made prominent a new form of denialism, more profound than those listed above. In late 2020, a poll found that some 56 per cent of Republicans believed the conspiracy theory was 'mostly or partly true'.[39] Although QAnon is still largely understood as a specific theory about the Democrats, over the course of the COVID-19 pandemic it mutated into a fundamental account of the whole world. Here, 'politics' becomes the conflict between evil elites and good elites and – given QAnon's ongoing hybridization with wellness culture – 'planet-healing vibes' vs 'demonic energy'. Neither incremental changes in atmospheric CO_2, nor the old denialist tropes of sunspots and natural cycles, can fit into this worldview because they don't – unlike everything else it conceives of – have a transparent moral character. Less extreme positions border this epistemic rift, such as those taken by various European far-right parties. These parties declare CO_2 'necessary for life', ascribing it a positive moral character and ignoring the matter of its concentration.[40] This same logic leads to the division of all biochemistry into 'masculinizing' and 'feminizing' components, as we discuss in the next chapter.

The Trump and Bolsonaro governments have been widely criticized for their inaction on, or even acceleration of, environmental problems. But this is not quite true. In climate change responses it is conventional to distinguish between mitigation and adaptation. 'Mitigation' refers to 'efforts to reduce or prevent emission of greenhouse gases', whereas 'adaptation' means 'adjustments in ecological, social, or economic systems in response to actual or expected climatic stimuli and their effects or impacts'.[41]

Far-right governments who reject the need for, or the possibility of, mitigation nevertheless pursue adaptation (in the form of securitization) as a major part of their programmes. Trump denied climate change, yet proposed building a US-Mexico border wall, which (according to the US military's own predictions) would be useful to stall future climate migration. Bolsonaro enhances the paramilitary powers of the police and installs military officers across his government. The trend appears across the global far right. Matteo Salvini, head of the far-right Lega, blocked migrant boats, their flight often induced by climate change, from docking in Italy. India has built a barbed wire fence along the Bangladesh/India border to protect against environmental refugees, with thousands of armed guards.[42]

In each case, a plausible response is made to climate change: not *as a climatic phenomenon*, but as a general social crisis requiring the imposition of an authoritarian state. The disease is denied and the symptoms (as they appear for the ruling class) are addressed. A self-terminating strategy, securitization might nevertheless be effective for the ruling class in the medium term. In this way, the US, Brazil, India, Australia and the EU already have their adaptation well underway.

Bruno Latour argued recently that Trump's withdrawal from the Paris Agreement shows that the American far right no longer thinks of itself as inhabiting the same earth as the rest of civilization.[43] But Latour's image misses that it is precisely on *this* planet that the far right fight for power, a planet of populations subject to massively differentiated risk and uneven governance: not the planet stylized as our common home, a 'pale blue dot' seen from Voyager I, but the actual planet, stratified by barbed wire and watched by the border police from a drone.

Non-denial denialism
(or, acceptance in one form or another)

Denialism is not the only force on the far right. Some have opted for various degrees of acceptance. Like denialism, this 'acceptance' is not one single thing. It can go in stages. The first stage of acceptance acknowledges something is wrong in the relation of humans to nature. But this acceptance is still almost entirely indeterminate. The second lays the blame with individualized consumption, often conspicuously commodified in the shape of consumer goods. The third stage entails a view of wider capitalist production that understands consumption not as individual greed but as a systemic effect of capitalism's demand for growth.

Even amongst the far-right 'acceptors', proposals for action, perspectives on the specific social and historical processes involved and even the central mechanics (increasing levels of atmospheric carbon being the most basic) of climate change are sometimes at odds with other environmentalists. Few adequately address the problem of global climate change, perhaps because little of their politics addresses that scale at all.

The European far-right party that has come closest to acceptance of climate change is France's National Rally (RN), now closer to executive power than at any time in its history. In 2017, Marine Le Pen moved to broaden her electoral campaign through environmentalism.[44] She argued for localizing production, as her denialist father and former RN leader had, but this time mentioned that it came with the added benefit of reducing emissions.[45] More strikingly, she claimed (as her father also had), that it was essential to fully close France's borders to migration. In the lead up to the European elections of 2019, the link between ecology and migration became a focus of RN's messaging: an RN spokesperson declared that, 'The best ally of ecology is the border'. Le Pen echoed this sentiment, declaring someone 'rooted in their home is an ecologist', whereas the 'nomadic . . . do not care about the environment'.[46] This arguably antisemitic framing of 'rootlessness' and indifference to nature was sourced from the writings of Hervé Juvin and the wider European New Right.

The environmental turn had begun in earnest in 2014 with the launch of the New Ecology movement. From the outset, it emphasized traditional far-right touchstones of 'family, nature and race', a continuation of politics from the party's founding in the 1970s.[47] It assumes the distinctness and fundamental incompatibility of different groups of people. Most radically different of all, it claims, are the Muslims. To maintain this diversity of peoples, everyone must be kept apart.

New Ecology rejected multilateral efforts on climate change, declaring the UNFCCC to be a 'communist project'. It advocated for the withdrawal of France from the Paris Agreement.[48] RN have voted in favour of having oil derived from Canadian tar sands as part of the EU fuel supply, yet opposes land wind turbines as 'sonic and aesthetic pollution'.[49] Some forms of renewable energy production are supported, such as nuclear power, which confers both environmental benefits and contributes to national energy security. As researcher Lise Benoist has written, for this form of far-right ecologism, the 'ultimate enemy is "the liberal-libertarian ideology" from which ensues the "the delirious globalist ecology"'. This delirious globalist ecology 'destroys landscapes through the construction of wind turbines and solar farms' and is 'determined to blame Europeans in order to better "deconstruct" their identities and traditions'.[50]

Elsewhere in Europe, Fidesz, the ruling party in Hungary, has had contradictory responses to climate change. It was the first EU party to ratify the Paris Climate Agreement and their MEPs have consistently supported climate action.[51] But this stance on the international stage is not reflected domestically, where environmental protection has been weakened.[52] Hungary has cut heavily the corporate tax rate, weakened labour laws severely and has caveated its commitments to both Paris and EU emission targets. Why? The need to protect automobile manufacturing powered by German capital. In 2018, Hungary's foreign minister stated the country would, 'never accept a proposal from Brussels that would hurt the German ... auto industry'. Notably, Hungary does not extract significant fossil fuels; its lax implementation of climate regulations is largely an appeal to foreign capital.[53]

Other far-right governments around the world have been no less mixed in their messages. Rodrigo Duterte of the Philippines, one of the most vulnerable countries in the world to climate change, declared his government would not honour its pledges under the Paris Agreement before insisting a mere week later that tackling climate change is his top priority.[54] The tension between these two statements is nevertheless comprehensible as a single strategy: Duterte objects to the injustice of being forced to curtail the industrialization of the Philippines while richer countries continue to emit greenhouse gases. He has further attempted to bolster his ecological credentials by chastising Canada for dumping waste in the Philippines. However, all of this matters little when under his watch death squads have run rampant in the country, suppressing Indigenous environmentalist movements opposed to governmental land grabs. In 2018, the Philippines was the most dangerous place in the world to be a land defender: 30 environmentalists were murdered. Since Duterte came to power, at least 119 have been killed.[55]

Along the Indus river lie the territorial claims of three nuclear powers: China (through Tibet), India (through Kashmir) and Pakistan. The river is at once one of the most important in the world, particularly for Pakistan, whose breadbasket region it irrigates, and runs through one of the most heavily contested territories in the world. Important components of Hindu nationalist politics are intimately tied up with control of the river and the wider Kashmir region. A series of hydroelectric dams constructed on the Indus by India have been contested by Pakistan, who claim it would allow India to shut off the flow of the river Pakistan relies on to grow crops, a potentially devastating geopolitical weapon. It is not yet clear how exactly climate change will change its flow, but undoubtedly its variability will increase.[56] This could lead to dangerous volatility in the region.

Into this complex situation steps Narendra Modi, Indian Prime Minister since 2014. Modi's ruling Bharatiya Janata Party (BJP) has positioned itself to defend the interests of Hindus at the expense of minorities. Modi's reputation was cemented by the pogrom against Muslims in Gujarat in 2002, where the official count documents 790 Muslims and 254 Hindus died (the real numbers are probably much higher). Some have claimed that Modi 'initiated, encouraged and condoned it'.[57] The pogrom in Gujarat was followed by violence against minorities in Orissa in 2007 and 2008 and in Muzaffarnagar in 2013.[58] What is the social function of these acts of violence? Anti-caste leader Dr. B.R. Ambedkar wrote in 1936 that 'a caste has no feeling that it is affiliated to other castes except when there is a Hindu-Muslim riot'. Class conflict (and caste conflict) in India are suppressed through the unification of the disparate groups in anti-Muslim violence.[59]

The second leader of the Rashtriya Swayamsevak Sangh (RSS), a large Hindu nationalist organization in India with close ties to the BJP, M.S. Golwalkar, who remains a major ideological touchstone for the group, argued that there were three enemies that imperil the Hindu nation: Muslims, Christians and Communists. These enemies are alike in one respect: 'they threaten to disrupt the supposedly "natural" unity and harmony of the Hindu race and Hindu civilization, which stretches back to time immemorial'. In

1939, he suggested that Nazi Germany was a good model for Hindu Nationalists to follow.[60] Some of the places where the RSS's vigilante 'moral policing' have been most prominent – such as 'cow defenders' who attack Muslims accused of eating or slaughtering cows, which is prohibited in Hinduism – concern the human relationship to a spiritualized nature.[61] Indeed, the growing vigilante militancy of the RSS, combined with its mobilization around stark religious and ethnic divisions, makes the situation in India arguably the closest in form to classical fascism of all countries of the contemporary period.

If the RSS and BJP are committed to the construction of a Hindu state, perhaps we should see Modi's environmental politics as intertwined with this project. Modi's report into Gujarat's response to climate change, published when he was Chief Minister, opens with a discussion of the *Rig Veda*, the oldest of the canonical Hindu texts. Modi points out that the '*Rig Veda* . . . emphasized on the importance [sic] of *Panch Tatvas* (five elements), earth, air, water, solar energy, and sky.' He goes on, 'any disproportionate use of these energies will cause pollution and will promote selfishness, instincts of violence, jealousy – inimical to human development'.[62] Elsewhere, Modi has called for 'special attention to yoga amidst discussions about climate change'.[63] Explaining climate change as a spiritual problem is not unique to Modi, but he is undoubtedly the most significant person to do so. How to understand these remarks? Jyoti Puri has argued that they 'derived from established discourses of Hindu spiritualism that were produced in opposition to, and as a remedy for, Western materialism'.[64]

In 2014, newly Prime Minister, he bordered on outright denial: 'Climate has not changed. We have changed. Our habits have changed . . . If we change, it [nature] is already ready to change. Humans should not struggle with the environment. Humans should love the environment. Be it water, air, plants.'[65] Similarly, as late as 2019, his environment minister denied that the devastating floods in the country were caused by climate change.[66]

Throughout Modi's premiership, environmental regulations have been scrapped. Some 99.82 per cent of industrial projects proposed in forests have been approved, up from 80 per cent.[67] In the midst of the COVID-19 pandemic, the government released plans to exempt 'coal mining, cement plants, chemical fertilizers, manufacturing of acids and pesticides' as well as those 'concerning national defence and security or other strategic considerations' from public consultation.[68] Pollution targets have been scrapped for power plants and, in the first half of 2016, sixteen new power plants went online without clean air technology installed.[69] The Modi government has also cracked down on environmental NGOs, in late 2014 blocking the flow of overseas funds to Greenpeace India because of 'anti-national' activities,[70] and in 2020 targeting Indian Fridays for Future activists.[71] It has pushed to further remove the protections put in place after the 1984 Bhopal disaster, in which thousands died and over half a million people were exposed to highly toxic chemicals.[72] This rapid development at the cost of environmental destruction is not unconnected to Modi's religious discourse: highways to pilgrimage sites have been driven through ecologically sensitive sites, in cases without compensation or consultation.[73]

Defenders of Modi might argue that rapid development is essential to help people escape the ravages of poverty. It is a potent argument. But environmental regulations largely defend those living in poverty, and the BJP has also shredded deliberative aspects of the state, where they can be heard. Here, neoliberal marketization and deregulation, as well as the dedemocratization of the state, go hand in hand with religiously inflected reactionary nature politics, which understands protestors as 'parasites'.[74]

There have, nevertheless, been some moves to mitigate climate change. The measures outlined in Modi's report from Gujarat are substantial. In 2014, Modi quintupled India's target for solar energy production by 2022 and then in 2015, on the eve of the Paris climate summit, India indicated for the first time a willingness to commit to legally binding emissions targets.[75] In 2015, Modi joined calls for a framework of 'Climate Justice'. Even here, religious discourse is intertwined: the call came at a Hindu-Buddhist conference where Modi proposed that Hinduism and Buddhism (although not Islam) were united in their ecological sensitivity.[76] In late 2020, India signalled its intention to intensify its mitigation efforts.[77]

What might we expect in the future? Given India's high risk of climate disruptions, the politics of adaptation are just as important as mitigation. There is a worrying possibility that the tendency towards social unification around anti-Muslim violence and exclusion will intersect in the future with climate change disasters. It is in this context that the 2019 amendment to the citizenship law, which provided a pathway for refugees claiming religious persecution in Afghanistan, Pakistan and Bangladesh, but not for Muslims, becomes relevant: it might allow for future denials of the citizenship of Muslims who cannot prove their status, and make it difficult to access disaster aid.[78] As Aranyo Aarjan writes, 'should a Hindu nationalist government which has shown a flagrant disregard for people's lives be in charge of the state of West Bengal, which has a sizeable impoverished Muslim population and shares a long border with the Muslim-majority Bangladesh, at a time when up to 18 million people will potentially be made into refugees by rising sea levels alone, the possible results are almost too bleak to consider.'[79]

Environmental authoritarianism

Interwar fascism mobilized frustration with the failures of democracy. The failings of the international order from the 1980s onwards in mitigating climate change might provide a formally similar justification for radical, unilateral action by others: geoengineering most of all, given its comparatively low cost and its ability to transform the global environment from anywhere.

This chapter has so far focused on those whose starting point is on the far right and subsequently confront the climate crisis. But the path in the opposite direction is also well-trodden: those already committed environmentalists who confront the enormity of the climate crisis and turn to authoritarian means. Some have argued that the greatest threat of 'eco-authoritarianism' can be found in the positions of mainstream technocratic 'green capitalist' environmentalists rather than amongst the far right.[80]

Arguments for authoritarian modes of governance have, in the past, come from within environmental movements. In the sometimes apocalyptic environmentalism of the 1970s, calls were made, most importantly by William Ophuls and Robert Heilbroner, for authoritarian regimes to solve the problem.[81] Garrett Hardin's arguments about the tragedy of the commons and lifeboat ethics also remain important touchstones for this trend of 'ecoauthoritarianism', and they are arguably all the more potent today. Although he published before the neoliberal atrophying of mass democratic life, Hardin assumes that the different users of a common resource can only be related economistically. He assumes the destitution of the social sphere of democratic negotiation and non-economic relationships *before it had actually come about in practice*. Tragically, through his call for the further privatization of the commons, he assisted the process which brought about its destitution.[82] If his tragedy of the commons model has utility, it is mostly for understanding the tragedy of the enforcement of its own recommendations.

There have been more recent calls for environmental authoritarianism. In 2015, Jørgen Randers, one of the authors of the 1972 Club of Rome report *The Limits to Growth*, proposed an 'enlightened dictatorship' in certain areas of policy to enact authoritarian measures that democratic electorates are unwilling to countenance. Randers cited ancient Rome and the Chinese Communist Party as examples of such an anti-democratic mechanism in practice.[83] In 2007, environmentalist David Shearman wrote of a need for an 'authoritarianism of experts' stating that 'absolute liberty cannot be preferable to life'.[84] In his *The Climate Challenge and the Failure of Democracy*, he advocated for an 'ecoelite' empowered to circumvent corporate interests.[85]

In truth, authoritarian governance does not equal effective governance.[86] Moreover, it has rarely in the past been anything other than profoundly destructive to the natural environment.[87] In a well-known 1978 article 'Leviathan, the Open Society and the Crisis of Ecology', David Orr and Stuart Hill refuted contemporary calls for an 'eco-authoritarian' state.[88] Authoritarian states cannot be expanded to meet some particular goal without expanding all other functions of the state as well. If we understand the state as a confluence of competing bureaucratic interests, then simply expanding state power will also heighten those contradictory impulses.

However, authoritarian states have changed since the late 1970s. Although certainly not far right in any conventional sense, it is in this context that China, viewed with fear and envy by the US and European far right, becomes essential to consider.[89] It plays two roles. First, it is a competitor nation for the US and Europe whose increasing standing seems to require a similarly escalatory response. The precise dynamics of this emerging so-called 'New Cold War' are, however, beyond the scope of this book. More directly important for us is China's transformation in appearance: over the last decade, it has attempted to present itself as an exemplary nation in the fight against climate change. The term 'Ecological Civilization' has been steadily incorporated into the official ideology of the state, making its way into the country's constitution in 2018.[90] In September 2020, Xi announced China would become carbon neutral by 2060 and called for a 'green recovery' in the aftermath of the COVID-19 pandemic.[91]

What do these promises have to do with authoritarianism? The concept of 'green control', explicated by Yifei Li and Judith Shapiro, names the use of 'technological surveillance tools',[92] used to implement environmental protection, 'also being used to assert and consolidate the hand of the state over individual and social groups'.[93] Not all this control is hi-tech: both mass campaigns and targeted crackdowns have long been a feature of Chinese governance, and their use has expanded to environmental measures.

The issue of pollution, in particular, has resulted in spectacular crackdowns by provincial governments unable, or unwilling, to differentiate between major and minor offenders. Smaller businesses have been harshly sanctioned while larger state-owned companies escape. This inconsistency of application at the local level nevertheless allows the central government to reaffirm its political legitimacy. Li and Shapiro argue that the multi-scalar nature of governance in China allows for the centre to step in, reimpose the order that local government has failed to justly enforce, and then leave again, allowing it to position itself as an 'impartial, uncorrupt environmental arbitrator in service to the Chinese people'.[94]

Similar dynamics between layers of government have played out elsewhere. In a poverty-stricken agricultural county in Henan in 2019, local officials, scrambling to meet emissions targets continuously monitored by automated air quality sensors, gave an unusual command: no machine harvesting this year. Use your hands instead. Why? Blooms of chaff from the wheat threshing machines were triggering the air monitoring system, and sending that data in real time back to the powerful Ministry of Ecology. The province would not meet its pollution targets. The harvest rotted. After irate farmers reported to journalists what had happened, officials for the province stepped in to denounce the local officials and the harvest resumed, too late to save the wheat.[95]

However, not all such measures are instigated by the state. The government has reacted quickly to public pressure on issues that damage the legitimacy of Communist Party rule, most importantly pollution. This responsiveness is deeply unequal. Relatively quick to engage with citizen's protests in affluent urban centres, it has neglected rural citizens.[96] More extremely, nomadic peoples living in China have been forcibly settled under the pretext of environmental control.

These geographical disparities affect the governance of environmental problems across the board. A significant part of China's drive towards 'Ecological Civilization' is a switch from coal power, on which China remains heavily reliant, to renewable energy, particularly hydroelectric power. Such a switch does not come without a cost. Historically, large water infrastructure projects have entailed mass involuntary resettlement, although resettlement practices have improved.[97]

The Belt and Road Initiative, a trillion-dollar communications, transportation and energy network, has allowed China to displace some of its environmental problems by relocating carbon-emitting industries from China to host countries[98] while precipitating new ecological disasters in areas of significant importance for biodiversity in Asia, Europe and Africa.[99] In poorer countries, environmental concerns have often been sidelined.

What does the example of China teach us? That environmentalism can be pursued without sacrificing forms of authoritarian control. Indeed, environmentalism, even at the large scales the European and US far right have typically shied away from, can be a mode through which authoritarianism is extended, and complex national security objectives achieved. However, the environmentalism this authoritarianism produces is characterized by superficiality, unevenness and, in some cases, the disingenuous displacement of carbon emissions, a process that China is on the receiving end of too.

But, the supporter of authoritarian action might object, faced with global climate systems breakdown, these criticisms are all so much chatter. Does it work? Is there less greenhouse gas in the atmosphere than there would be otherwise? It remains to be seen how significantly China can cut its emissions. Early signs are mixed. In early 2021, for example, it announced its 14th Five Year Plan, which contained no clear plan for phasing out coal.[100] Indeed, 'dozens of [coal-fired] power plants currently are under construction or planned'. Despite plans to reach peak emissions by 2030, further cuts than are planned will be needed to reach carbon neutrality by 2060, although this problem also besets responses worldwide.[101]

Comparative research indicates that democracies tend to lessen carbon emissions more effectively than authoritarian states, when they are free of corruption.[102] Might arguments for less democracy and more authoritarianism hold water in the West? Here we might return to Wendy Brown and, using her critique of neoliberalism, suggest that the problem climate change mitigation has so far faced has not been an excess of democracy, but rather democracy put in the cage of neoliberalism. Not an excess of democracy, but the slow atrophying of it to periodic elections for administrators of an unchangeable order.[103]

Other paths to climate change mitigation run more compellingly not towards authoritarianism, but towards deliberative input from the public, and greater democratization.[104] These deliberative processes do not suffer from a lack of public knowledge, but actually construct it. One recent study found that 'providing US citizens with the opportunity to engage in deliberation resulted in increased awareness regarding climate change and greater trust in science, technology, and international agreements'.[105]

Nor are the outputs of deliberative democracy short-termist or unambitious. A recent French public deliberative process on climate change concluded with a highly ambitious plan to tackle climate change directly, which was subsequently watered down by the Macron government.[106] Not the grotesque and short-sighted failure of an ignorant public, then, but the failure of a system still all too impervious to democratic control.

We have seen the governmental far right responding to the challenge of climate change in different ways. Some, such as Bolsonaro and Trump, gleefully dismantle environmental legislation while deepening securitization. Some displace 'green' politics into matters of national culture and landscape, while dismissing much of the multilateral requirements of mitigation. Some moralize climate change, presenting care for the environment as a religiously differentiated capacity. And some, such as China, not directly connected to the far right, utilize forms of environmental authoritarianism to increase unaccountable power in ways that are increasingly tempting for those with authoritarian instincts, but which we argue do not present a viable path.

Next, we examine the second part of the three-way split we identified above: far-right movements. We ask how ideas of nature in these movements are changing, and reckon with their capacity to grow into a widespread common-sense nature politics, as they would hope to.

3

Online far-right ecologism and far-right movements

In mid-2020, one confused poster wrote on the image-board 8kun, the successor website to 8chan, where two self-described 'ecofascist' terrorists had posted their manifestos: 'Where the fuck did everyone go?' Came the reply: 'The chans are dying anon . . . I suggest you train, pick up a book or begin to organize IRL [in real life] now. Just know that those of us who really understood what we had before it was destroyed will always miss you as well. We shared something unique.'[1]

Although the whimpering online end of the entity known as the 'alt-right' – a large, broadly online far-right movement instrumental to the election of Trump – came in 2020, the movement had been in inexorable decline since late 2017, when a member of the alt-right murdered an anti-fascist protestor at a rally in Charlottesville. It had encountered various external limits: its collapsing utility to Trump, declining political novelty and the tightening of moderation policies on major internet platforms. To these it had responded chaotically, reflecting its pronounced ideological heterogeneity. Nevertheless, many aspects of it persist. Its declining importance for mass online politics should not be taken as a final goodbye, but more as a mutation into another form, the precise character of which has yet to be settled.

Heterogeneity had been helpful to the alt-right. Its multi-facetedness had allowed it to absorb and deflect criticism: when it wasn't using it as proof of its own cultural relevance, it could deflect criticism by pointing to some other contrasting facet. When it could maintain its extremely high velocity, internal ideological conflict hadn't mattered so much – it was going so fast and seemed to many observers so novel that it avoided the need to explain itself.

However, the events of late 2017 and 2018 (during which it complicated its previously laudatory relationship with Trump) signalled a decline. Further complications and splits emerged through a series of events: the Christchurch mosque attack, the 2020 US election, and the rise of QAnon. The 'metapolitical' currents of the alt-right dissolved into a multitude of distinct subcultures. An incomplete list of these splits reads as follows: Traditional Catholicism, neopaganism, ecofascism, fashwave, esoteric Hitlerism, SIEGE, flea, terrorwave, pine tree, trad masculinism, Pepe revivalists, antisemitic Bitcoin maximalism, conventional White Nationalism, racial Americanism, groyper army, and even the dregs of NRx.[2] Each operated in its own cultural space. Each responded to the collapse of the alt-right by attempting to ground it in some *other* deeper project.

For some, the core of the alt-right turned out to *always have been* a particular relation of whiteness to nature. Unlike the governmental far right, they don't have to show how they would govern society, nor how they would reproduce capitalist social relations. They don't have to explain how they would secure national security, govern energy systems or allocate scarce resources. Accordingly, their figurations of 'nature' are broader, encompassing disquisitions on masculinity, the wilderness, spiritualism, food, 'conspirituality', neo-paganism, primitivism, a simplified and purified 'metapolitics', various forms of reactionary 'drop out' culture, modernity as such, the left's failure to break with capitalism and their promise to do just that. Where nature is invoked, it is more often than not as a regulatory norm for how humans should behave rather than indicative of a sustained interest in the natural world. 'Climate change' is present as a generic apocalypse, the content of which turns out often to have a distinctly racial character: the apocalypse as the end of racial history, as the slow degradation of racial potency and purity by capitalist 'excess'.

These movements as a whole might be understood as a reaction to facets of 'neoliberal environmentalism'. Neoliberalism has entailed the destruction of workers' organizations across the Global North and the atrophying of mass associational politics more generally. The move-mentist far right thus responds chiefly not to an imminent communist threat (as it believed it did in the 1920s and 1930s) but to the more steady march of social liberalization (support for which has spread across swathes of economic and political life). Neoliberal environmentalism entails the individualization of responsibility: buying a Tesla, offsetting your holiday by planting some trees, eating at a locally sourced restaurant and so on.[3] The attempt to break out of these trivialities has spurred the actions of some small far-right groups in the 'identitarian' tradition.

Identitarian youth movements have been linked directly to some of the mainstream parties discussed above, as well as to the terrorists in the following chapter.[4] Their politics venerates youth (a common refrain declares a 'war on the baby boomers') and blames past generations for ecological crises. In this generational framing, ecological degradation crisis fits snugly with the overriding concern of identi-tarians, the supposed 'extinction' of white Europeans. In both, the blame lies with preceding generations who have passed down their apocalyptic sins for the youth to suffer: a deracinated people, a scarred and exploited landscape, and perhaps most importantly, a slobbish, all-too-comfortable generation of men.

The now-defunct American Identity Movement (AIM), summarized its environmentalism in one of its sticker campaigns: 'Plant more trees, save the seas, deport refugees'. Whereas alt-right leader Richard Spencer's Alt-Right Manifesto had hedged in 2017 on the 'climate controversy',[5] AIM and groups like them were freer to express more direct environmental commitments as the alt-right dissolved.

Politically similar to identitarianism, but outside its formal alliances, lies CasaPound Italia (CPI). The group draws eclectically on political, tactical and aesthetic traditions outside the far right (most notably setting up a network of squatted social centres) to expand its influence.[6] Environmentalism is expressed most clearly through CPI's La Foresta Che Avanza (The Advancing Forest) which incorporates a tree-planting programme. This event is timed yearly for the 'Festival of the Tree', originally spearheaded by Mussolini's brother. It fetishizes native plant life supposedly under threat from invasive alien species, a construction reflected in CPI's extreme anti-migrant politics.[7]

Golden Dawn, once the most powerful far-right street movement in Europe, is now largely defunct, declared a criminal organization by the Greek courts, and its leadership imprisoned or in hiding. Distinguishable from much of the European far right by its open pro-violence stance, it patrolled areas where migrants lived, intervened as 'racial vigilantes' and was connected to attacks on immigrants and political enemies. Violence gave the party its coherence and identity.[8]

Like CPI, Golden Dawn's Green Wing tied the environment to race: 'Our love for nature is different than theirs [the left]: The environment is the cradle of our Race, it mirrors our culture and civilization, making it our duty to protect it.' Landscape became a proxy for Greek civilization and Greekness. When Greece was struck by forest fires, Green Wing organized volunteer firefighters and promoted reforestation. Such campaigns sought to 'restore the harmony between the Greeks and the nature [sic]'. GMO crops are despised. Green Wing objected to 'the replacement of many local productive plants by mutated seeds [from] Monsanto and other multinationals'. These crops, they argued, would cause 'the extinction of the indigenous wildlife' and 'lead to the eradication of any chance we have to achieve national independence and nutritional autarchy'.[9] Monsanto entailed an insupportable dependency on something beyond the nation state. Issues of energy and resource extraction were also framed as national concerns. Golden Dawn rejected renewable energy and instead proposed the nationalization and expansion of fossil fuel extraction, with the profits saved for ethnic Greeks.[10] But Green Wing was also more radical than most other groups. Amongst littering campaigns and fighting forest fires was a partially-developed Greeks-only blood bank programme,[11] reminiscent of the arbitrary racial distinctions made in the Nazi's blood programme.[12]

The 'environmental' focus of these two organizations is rarely on climate change but instead on local issues: invasive species, animal rights, littering, pollution, landscape protection and so on.[13] Nature politics here is thus a combination of metaphysical unity (CPI and Green Wing both assert the integrity of people and land) and highly specific and well-known components of nature. Spiritual unity with the land is expressed through defending symbolic aspects of the local ecology, often starting with national food culture and charismatic megafauna. Environmentalism is present, but subordinated to the primary political messaging: anti-leftism, anti-liberalism, the hatred of migrants and the preservation of 'race'.

Quite another tendency, deploying similar ideas, has appeared in the US. In November 2020, Mike Peinovich, host of the podcast 'The Daily Shoah', founded the National Justice Party (NJP). 'Third Positionist' in strategy, the party attempted to appeal to disillusioned leftists. Its programme declares: 'The state must act as the steward of the environment. Industrial and economic needs will be balanced with quality of life and the preservation of natural beauty . . . religious slaughter and other inhumane treatment of animals will be banned.'[14] Such a mix of positions is meant to resolve the contradictions between competing interest groups that Third Positionism attempts to appeal to: blue-collar workers, racists, 'environmental patriots' and disaffected leftists.

Even more explicitly aimed at the left was the speech given by Warren Balogh, one of the other chairmen of the party. He rejected the 'marketing slogan' of action on carbon emissions, suggesting that 'pollution, deforestation, habitat degradation, overexploitation, or urban sprawl', had been deliberately sidelined. He called for 'those environmentalists . . . who know that globalization is the problem' to give up on their 'fake democratic socialism'. What other form of socialism was Balogh proposing? His description of a 'corpulent [fat] neoliberal Jew . . . with a very high squeaky voice' advocating for increased immigration and of Kamala Harris as 'a creature of Jew finance' might give us some clues: Balogh was proposing National Socialism.[15]

In the UK, another connection to land and nature has been asserted. On 9 August 2020, coinciding with the UN's Indigenous People's Day, a series of banner drops were organized across nationally significant locations in the UK by Patriotic Alternative (PA), a new political party positioning itself as a successor to the British National Party (BNP). The banners declared 'White Lives Matter'. PA's point was clear: white Britons were the 'indigenous' people of the British Isles and, under the same threats as indigenous peoples elsewhere, and thus due the same protections.[16] The same language of indigeneity had previously been used by Nick Griffin, then leader of the BNP, on his appearance on the BBC's flagship current affairs panel show, *Question Time*, in 2009: 'No one [would] dare . . . go to North America and say to an American Red Indian [sic] "what do you mean indigenous?" We're all the same'.

Appropriating indigeneity discourse is not limited to the UK. The figure of the 'Native American', confined to their reservation, has been used across the European far right, including by La Lega, Alternative für Deutschland (AfD) and the Swiss Democrats, to warn of the fate of White Europeans if non-white immigration is not halted.[17] This indigeneity discourse is a rhetorical tool rather than a commitment to indigenous rights writ large. And for the European far right, the label is badly misapplied. 'Indigeneity' is a political category which depends on a power imbalance with a colonizing power. It is not simply the term for occupying a particular piece of land.[18] In truth, as with those right-environmentalists discussed earlier, the wealth that the far right equates with their advantageous racial character is itself a product of the suppression and destruction of indigenous and colonized peoples worldwide.

These projects – Generation Identity, CasaPound Italia, Golden Dawn's Green Wing, the National Justice Party, Patriotic Alternative – are spaces of comparative coherence in the wider far right's articulation of nature. Yet each project tells of the distinct inadequacy of the national scale when addressing environmental issues. The localized destruction of particular environments is treated as a scandalous affront to natural limits, while the structural condition of carbon emissions goes largely unremarked, or even vociferously defended.

There is one important exception: the youth wing of the Alternative für Deutschland (Junge Alternative für Deutschland, or JA). The group has extremist tendencies, even for the AfD, and the party leadership has considered dissolving it.[19] While the older AfD has been one of the most consistently denialist groups on the far right (it has claimed that Greta Thunberg is merely the 'face of [a] covert, pre-planned public relations campaign run by the international left'),[20] the JA have shown more willingness to accept the reality of climate change, demanding the party change course on climate change after a poor showing in the European Parliament elections.[21] The intervention did not succeed. The wider party continued to be denialist.

These groups are limited in scale. But even these groups have more of a relation to concrete environment-making practices than do the following subcultures, which act as 'laboratories' for forms of reactionary nature politics. Developed away from popular attention, such conceptions of nature nevertheless have the capacity to develop into important viable subcultures with widespread impact. Though small now, we suggest that we will retrospectively realize how important the configuration of 'nature' in the nebulous, ill-defined spaces of the online far right is.

Ted 'Unabomber' Kaczynski memes are shared as cornerstones of a worldview. In networks of Telegram channels (an instant messaging app popular on the far right), self-described 'ecofascists' prepare for race war and the collapse of society. Far-right intellectuals trying to play the long game of metapolitics end up arguing for an increase in child mortality. Self-appointed shamans practice energy healing and campaign for the overthrow of the deep state. And disaffected men band together in hierarchical 'wolf packs' to venerate their ancestors and drop out of society. Is a distinct ideology of nature identifiable in the online far right? Such memetic chaos defies easy summarization but it consistently combines refusal of a world they see as beset by degeneracy, race mixing and consumerism with exhortations to brutally enforce traditional gender roles and strive for racial honour, purity and purpose. Sometimes, this means dropping out.

In *Harassment Architecture*, a book heavily promoted on 'ecofascist' Telegram channels, the author, Mike Ma, urges his readers to adventurism: 'Quit your job and sit in the sun every day. Quit your job and run away into the woods forever. Quit your job and shoot a politician.'[22] But it's not so easy to break with normality: 'I'm aware that by the time I've driven out to a sizable piece of land with all the necessary tools to survive that I'll lose the ambition to follow that feeling.'[23] The response to this incoherence? Further radicalization. But it is not the radicalism of these arguments that should give us pause so much as their strangely incoherent juxtapositions of disparate parts. One meme posted on a now-deleted 'ecofascist' Telegram channel depicted an AK-47-armed man silhouetted against the neo-Nazi 'black sun' symbol and urged its viewers to 'fight the System'. The proposed methods? 'Eating less fast food' and 'recycling'. The nature politics that emerges from this wing of the far right is still, as we hope to show, fundamentally inadequate for thinking about our future, or ever engaging with climate change at a sufficient scale. It is both repugnant and trivial, although its danger is that neither will limit its spread.

As environmentalism has become more popular generally and therefore heterogeneous, this complexity has been used by some on the far right to produce rifts of uncertainty within environmentalism more broadly. In one such case, pairs of stickers, widely disseminated throughout the UK by the Hundred Handers organization, grotesquely misrepresented the politics of Extinction Rebellion (XR) as punitive and masochistic: 'Live in a shed/Give your house to an African', read the first. The other, seemingly in response, read 'Sink the boats/Save the world', equating the murder of migrants with the fight against climate change. Whether 'the world' was to be understood as the exclusively white lifeworld of an imagined UK or the global climate overburdened with CO_2 was perhaps unclear: the danger perhaps lies in the conflation of the two.

Others pretended to be XR chapters on Twitter, posting in the first wave of the COVID-19 pandemic that 'Corona is the cure. Humans are the disease!'[24] Other groups, for example Local Matters in the UK, have attempted to gain metapolitical traction by posing as inoffensive environmental organizations. Formed by former members of the far-right Generation Identity UK, their purported ideology – their asininely stated 'Localism' – combines ethnonationalism with calls for better public transport.[25]

Perhaps aware of this general disconnection between rhetoric and programme, Richard Spencer, one of the most important figures in the alt-right, has called for the far right to develop an avatar-politics around the climate, utilizing a single charismatic figurehead (a kind of right-wing Greta Thunberg) to express the alt-right's 'naturalist' politics.[26] He, too, thinks there is a 'crisis in the natural world', but is less concerned with how it might be articulated – as climate change or – more 'poetically' – as the critique of pervasive 'ugliness'. Unconcerned with specifics, he nevertheless remains confident: 'only we [the alt-right] can solve this problem'.[27] But the existent far right already has many prominent voices on nature politics, if not climate change. Their articulations of nature are many and varied, but circle almost without fail around the figure of the individual man. This masculinist turn integrates scepticism about modernity, veneration of a Nietzschean will-to-power and self-help literature.

Bronze Age Pervert (BAP) is one of the most distinctive voices in far-right politics. His book *Bronze Age Mindset* is a Nietzschean exhortation to action, which celebrates the supposedly daring and exceptional, an exceptionality rooted in a quasi-spiritual biological superiority. Condemning Darwinism as 'bug-thought', BAP invokes the Ancient Greek idea of Nemesis: 'In nature there is irrepressible force . . . Its destruction of the feeble designs of reason, the pointless words of man – this is beautiful.'[28] Such romantic anti-rationalism is redolent of interwar fascist propaganda. Again and again BAP attempts to distil transhistorical glory from violence. Robert Denard, a mercenary and coup-leader BAP characterizes as 'defending whatever residues of civilization remained in Africa after decolonization', and the mercenary Mad Mike Hoare, are celebrated as latter-day incarnations of the spirit of the Spartan general Brasidas.[29] In truth, mercenaries such as these were funded by 'colonial interests who wanted to remain influential in their old stomping grounds';[30] not romantic 'pirates' outside of the empire, but enforcers of its brutal frontier logic.

Elsewhere, BAP declares that 'the "liberation" of women makes democracy into a terminal disease . . . one that doesn't just end a particular government, but the civilization.'[31] His most important figure – the 'bugman', who is 'motivated by a titanic hatred of the well-turned-out and beautiful' – comes in for the sharpest criticism when his despoliation of the environment is connected to a panoply of modern degeneracies: 'The bugman seeks to bury beauty under a morass of ubiquitous ugliness and garbage. ... The waters are polluted with birth control pills and mind-bending drugs emitted by obese high-fructose-corn-syrup-guzzling beasts.' Such disgusting visions of the world confer on a chosen few (those who wield the power of 'Nemesis') the right to fight against this tide of mediocre ugliness. It is also a moment, apparent across the right, in which consumption itself (feminized in the form of the 'birth control pills') is seen as luring one into obedience. The opposite of this feminized figure of compulsive consumption is the 'cottagecore tradwife', whose modesty and contentedness repudiates all modern excess. Moments later, the hatred is for migrants: 'dwarf-like zombies are imported for slave labor and political agitation from the fly-swept latrines of the world'.[32] His book is perhaps the most significant in the online subcultures of the far right, supported by a viral marketing campaign of anonymized bodybuilders reading it in public. From there, BAP's words found their way, reportedly, to prominent advisors in the Trump White House.[33]

Naturalized masculinism also comes in the spate of far-right fighting clubs, both in the UK and US,[34] and the 'ecofascist bare-knuckle fighting' popular on Telegram.

However, assertions of virility *sui generis* are ultimately, and conspicuously, shallow. The body is involved in an exchange with the outside. And it is the control of this exchange around which many of the most conspiratorial aspects of far-right nature politics flow. Across the breadth of the post-alt-right, the same idea is repeated: nature makes our bodies; degenerate nature makes degenerate people. Here, the concept of nature expands to include flows of molecules. Two online tributary cultures to the contemporary far right – incels and bodybuilding culture[35] – mix crude biology, diet advice (36 eggs and two multivitamins a day), and sometimes dangerous surgery in the pursuit of the perfect masculine body. Wider conspiracy culture also plays on anxieties about masculinity and the control of one's chemical intake: Alex Jones, host of the globally popular *InfoWars* show, makes much of his money through the sale of 'uniquely pure' dietary supplements.[36] Bodybuilding and conspiracy culture's concern for perfection and purity become, on the far right, a disgust for all that is impure.

Masculinity becomes intimately related to the politics of the consumption of nature. The 'soyboy' is a figure of derision, whose consumption of soy and its attendant 'xenoestrogens' leads them to enjoy contemporary commodities and thus effeminizes them. It is perhaps fitting that soybeans are neoliberalism's 'growth crop'.[37] The idea here, exactly because of its triviality, is more radical: the idea that the government wants to control you is a less radical conspiracy than that people enjoy eating soy. The former only requires that you oppose the government; the latter implies the whole social fabric is degenerate.[38] This aversion to uncontrolled chemical flows is redolent of the anxieties of the Freikorps detailed by Klaus Theweleit in *Male Fantasies*.[39]

However, consumption is played both ways. Where left-environmentalists might advocate vegetarianism or veganism, for some on the far right, eating meat is a symbol of potency, of communion with nature. Mike Ma again: 'I see God in raw meat. I see God in rare meat'.[40] Or, more ridiculously, one viral stunt saw white nationalists quaff huge quantities of milk to prove their genetic right to the cattle-grazing lands of Europe and America.[41]

The complex interactions of real molecules and their involvements with power[42] are reduced to two functions: virilization and emasculation. This binary is reflected in the well-worn internet parlance of 'alpha and beta', 'virgin and chad'. This simplicity does not assuage anxiety but seems to deepen it. Because degeneracy is such an unclear and changeable category and homosocial violence is so common in these spaces, only the most consistently maintained hyper-masculine stance will suffice as a defence against the accusation of degeneracy.

One systematization of far-right theories of the left is 'bioleninism'. Those that the left appeals to today are a biological underclass: 'Women. Homosexuals. Transexuals. Muslims. Blacks. There's even movements propping up disabled and fat people.'[43] What we learn from these is that the left has become, in the eyes of the far right, not a political movement, but a biological one. Similarly, BAP approvingly praises Mad Mike Hoare for understanding 'communism for what it was: the infestation of vermin he was tasked to exterminate, a biological event, not an ideological, political, or historical one'.[44]

Purity and fear of impurity are also two of the major aesthetic themes of the burgeoning movement called 'conspiratualism' (a portmanteau of 'conspiracy' and 'spiritualism'), the most important part of which is QAnon. These movements have two core convictions: '(1) a secret group covertly controls, or is trying to control, the political and social order, and (2) humanity is undergoing a "paradigm shift" in consciousness.'[45] These conspiritualist beliefs in and of themselves are not far right. However, the political indeterminacy of such claims leaves them open to such appropriations, not least antisemitic ones. Some have suggested that any 'articulation of current conspiracy theories is to evoke political positions on the extreme right, wittingly or not'.[46] Certainly the integration of QAnon into the wider far right has been accelerating even as the movement differentiates into distinct parts, more or less concerned with spiritual purity.

With the same religious drive, but a greater explicitness in its connection to the far right is a particular strand in neo-paganism. A (relatively) recent construction, neo-paganism provides for its far-right adherents a belief system free from the influence of the 'Abrahamic' (read 'Jewish') religions. For American white nationalists, living in a land where they can claim no long history, paganism allows a deep connection to the land to be asserted. 'Vinland', the name Viking explorers gave to the part of North America on which they landed, features prominently in North American white nationalist paganism.[47]

Neo-paganism has spawned 'back to the land' racial communes. 'How much more useful it would be', Jost Turner, the founder of one such commune, wrote of the wider far right, 'to put their energy into hewing themselves a homestead, and ultimately an Aryan community . . . Why not take up the old hippy slogan to "drop out", and begin by destroying this anti-white system by non-participation?' Here, nature becomes a refuge from the vagaries of degenerate modernity. For Wyatt Kaldenberg, an editor of the newspaper *Pagan Revival* and contributor to *White Aryan Resistance*, nature was, conversely, hostile to the white race. Christianity, which he characterized as an alien religion, had alienated the white race from its own gods and introduced demobilizing ideas of pacifism and non-aggression.[48] To recover their compact with nature, white people had, he suggested, to become pagans.

Less radical than these pagan visions, but also in stark and forceful opposition to the debt-sustained 'disciplinary hedonism' of mass commodity consumption, some on the far right attempt to enter into other past utopias, most frequently postwar America. In truth, this was a moment of the massive expansion of consumerism.[49] In these images of the past, however, social change is almost always presented as exogenous: it is never the product of internal contradictoriness or tension.

These attempts to 'return' have even inflected contemporary overpopulation discourse, which has moved broadly from the problem of 'too little civilization' to 'too much'. Even after the apocalyptic pronouncements of 1970s neo-Malthusianism did not come to pass, the idea of overpopulation persisted. We might suggest that the new forms of overpopulation discourse are stimulated either by the wish to contain life or by an assertion of scarcity as an ontological principle. Stronger still: as a principle of justice. There *should* be scarcity, some neo-Malthusians of the far right seemingly say. In conversation with Richard Spencer, the writer Edward Dutton claimed that the historic drop in infant mortality over the last few hundred years has reduced the effectiveness of environmental selection. According to Dutton, reducing infant mortality leads to higher 'mutational load', which he reports can cause such horrors as atheism, left-handedness and left-wing politics.[50] In response, Dutton argues for the reimposition of 'Darwinian conditions' of 50 per cent child mortality. What he proposes is appalling but it also evidences a poor grasp of evolutionary theory. Humans live in all different kinds of environments. Some in cities, some in rainforests, some in tundra. No one of these is – or can be – uniquely or specifically 'Darwinian'.[51]

Dutton's work, whatever its peculiarity, fits within a broader shift in population discourse from 'too little civilization' to 'too much'.[52] In contemporary transformations of limit-discourse more generally, 'consumption and not population per se . . . is foregrounded . . . shifting the concern of governance from managing savage life and its tendency to overpopulation, to managing life in general'.[53]

What explains this attachment to scarcity? Perhaps here the far right is not so far from neoliberalism. As Andrew Ross wrote already in 1996,

> for more than two decades now, public consciousness has sustained complex assumptions about both kinds of scarcity. In that same period of time, however, neo-liberalism's austerity regime has ushered in what can only be described as a pro-scarcity climate, distinguished, economically, by deep concessions and cutbacks and, politically, by the rollback of 'excessive' rights. As a result, the new concerns about natural scarcity have been parallelled, every step of the way, by a brutal imposition of social scarcity.[54]

Here as well, the far right acts to exemplify the tendencies of neoliberalism, not contradict them.

If civilization has become *too much*, then how should we respond? In Jack Donovan's fantasy of a group of men poised on the edge of survival,[55] in Edward Dutton's call for reinstating 'Darwinian conditions', and in the Greenline Front's call for 'the deification of Nature, which has been lost due to semitization [becoming more Jewish] of [the] inner world of the Europeans',[56] natural conditions are repeatedly presented as something that modernity has obscured. In each example, we find the tension between *a natural irrepressible eternal truth* and *the desperate need to act in a radical fashion to recover it* that animates far-right nature politics. Sometimes, cyclical notions of historical time, in which the present is the fallen moment before the resurrection of the Golden Age, are deployed to explain such inconsistencies.[57]

We might even suggest that these beliefs amount to primitivism.[58] Variants of political primitivism typically invert negative aspects of the society their proponents live in. Contemporary society is an immensely complex and multifaceted phenomenon and, accordingly, contemporary primitivism's inversions of it are diverse. Some proponents, such as John Zerzan, invert our hyper-technological and unequal society into utopian hunter-gatherer societies, technologically simple and ostensibly extremely equal.[59] Right-wing proponents invert modernity's cultural diversity and global infrastructure into ethnically homogeneous agrarian communities structured around deeply felt customs, hierarchical relationships, integrity of life with the land, and fiercely and physically defended private property. The Bronze Age Pervert's central concept is 'owned space', an idea that overlays the notion of a physically commanded space of ethnic identity onto the libertarian primacy of property rights.

Is primitivism a kind of nihilism? Brown has argued compellingly that neoliberal subject construction lays the groundwork for the nihilism pervasive on the contemporary right.[60] On the far right, the transformation moves one step further from nihilism into absolute conspiratorial affirmation. However, in a world systematized by huge and distinctly 'impure' historical forces such as capitalism, what can be affirmed unproblematically by those concerned with purity is a minuscule slice of existence: everything else – namely, almost all of civilization – must be destroyed or abandoned for the purpose of the preservation of this absolute pure single thing.

Such far-right primitivists don't view climate change as a particular event in the history of the environment or in the history of capitalism, but as a consequence of a far broader problem: 'industrial society' in the terminology of Ted Kaczynski, or even everything inside 'agricultural society'. The politics becomes fatalistic: all that is left is an escape to the woods, but even that will likely fail.

This feeling of enclosure, of the breakdown of possibility, is also expressed in the forms of far-right nature politics which kill people. The alt-right, lacking formal organization, both encouraged violence and was unable to prevent it when it began to threaten its very existence. It is this proliferation of far-right terrorists, invoking in some cases the ideas of far-right nature politics, to which we turn now.

4
Deadly ecofascist violence

On 15 March 2019, a gunman entered the Al Noor Mosque in Christchurch, New Zealand, and shot 42 people dead. Six minutes later, he got back into his car and drove to the Linwood Islamic Centre, where Abdul Aziz Wahabzada, a worshipper at Friday prayers, made a heroic attempt to confront and distract the attacker. By the end of the bloodshed the gunman had killed 51 people, all Muslim, torn apart innumerable lives and his manifesto had spread across the internet. He called himself an 'ecofascist'.

In the manifesto, many of the trends we have mapped in the previous chapters crystallize: the intensely conspiratorial aspects of far-right thinking; the potent mix of islamophobia and antisemitism; a fanatical attention to racial purity; the need to respond with overwhelming violence; a neo-Malthusianism in the form of fantasies of 'racial replacement' as a fundamental ecological issue; and a bloodthirsty fanaticism.

Despite its virality, the manifesto was not intended to appeal to a large audience. The shooter mentions the need to gather a young audience with 'edgy humour and memes'. The text is riddled with internet jokes and niche far-right references and is composed as a mish-mash of polemical theses, Q&As, poetry and exhortation to action. References to previous far-right terrorists reveal its intention: to spur others to similar acts. In this it succeeded.

In August of the same year, another gunman walked into a Walmart in El Paso, US, and killed 23 people, mostly Latino or Latina. He too called himself an 'ecofascist', and placed himself in the lineage of previous mass killers. What's most astonishing about the El Paso shooter's manifesto is the lack of ideological justification. Between the surprisingly measured critique of immigration policy – it has the tone of a somewhat unengaged high-school paper – and the act of shooting people of colour randomly in a Walmart lies a gulf of justification.

Part of an attempted bridge – however incomplete it must remain – must be the extreme sense of political impossibility that had seemingly motivated both shooters. Both had 'taken the black pill', an extension of the 'red pill/blue pill' logic first found in the Wachowskis' film *The Matrix*. The blue pill takes you back to the regular world, the red pill allows you to see the reality behind appearances (on the far right, the reality and centrality of race), but the black pill is something beyond these two. It not only inverts reality; it affirms that there is no solution in mainstream politics. Other means must be sought.

The most arresting moment in the Christchurch shooter's manifesto comes not in its discussion of the environment but in the repeated opening declaration: 'It's the birth rates'. 'Demographic change' is the apocalypse-to-come, not climate change. The argument goes like this: birth rates among white people in countries in the Global North are declining. Meanwhile, birth rates among migrant populations are higher. The shooter extrapolated directly from these two trends to argue that the white populations of the world are destined to become extinct, ignoring important demographic trends like the tendency of birth rates to decline after migration to wealthier countries.

This racial population thinking is not specific to the blackpilled. The conspiracy theory it stems from is called

'The Great Replacement', which was the title of the Christchurch shooter's manifesto. It has many iterations – with or without antisemitic elements, with a variety of different 'replacing' populations, as well as a variety of different proposed solutions. Antisemitic versions of the theory believe that the 'replacement' is being orchestrated by Jews. Others believe that the Jews are one of the groups being replaced, along with other Europeans, by Arabs.[1] This variety enables it to function as a common underlying conspiracy theory, accepted with slight variations, for much of the far right.

Proponents of the 'Great Replacement' often imagine non-whites as strongly ethnocentric, even capable of operating as a single, unified bloc. Sometimes, this is presented as an alliance of everyone else against white people, or just one particular group (in Europe, this is typically Muslims). It is this supposed capacity for highly coordinated collective action that produces the most intense fever dreams of the far right. When they become the majority, some versions of the conspiracy claim, non-white people will start to use their majority status to deny white people the right to vote, or even to intern them in concentration camps. One needn't be a psychoanalyst to suggest that such fantasies of aggression are the far right's own intentions, projected.

What constitutes the category of 'white' in this conspiracy? There is no single definition, but two examples from the history of such classifications importantly give very different pictures. Purists tend to adopt the 'one-drop rule', which makes whiteness both fragile and irrecoverable. Other classificatory systems for whiteness, such as Apartheid South Africa's, which conferred whiteness onto people if they were either physically 'obviously white' or socially understood as white, yield very different demographic predictions. These different classification systems speak to different forms of racism: biological and degenerative in the former (whiteness can only decline) and mutable and social in the latter. Such definitions are arbitrary: in the past, neither the Italian nor the Irish were regarded as white, and the classification of Polish people still remains contested for parts of the far right.[2]

Inflecting the 'Great Replacement' conspiracy with fears of natural extinction, the short-lived far-right group Greenline Front described its politics as 'not only for the preservation of all kinds of animals and plants, but also against the extinction of the White Man!'[3] Nor is the fear of racial or group extinction confined to any one part of the far right: Neoreactionaries, very different beasts indeed, have argued that cities, particularly city states like Singapore, may be productive in the short term, but in the long run function as 'IQ-shredders'. Misreading the higher IQ of urban populations as a biological fact rather than understanding it as related to the process of urbanization, they argue that urban populations' lower fertility rates are ultimately dysgenic.[4]

If its main fixation was on demographic change, what then is the environmentalist content of the Christchurch shooter's 'ecofascist' manifesto? The question is directly asked and answered in the Q&A portion of the manifesto: 'Europeans', he writes, 'are one of the groups that are not overpopulating the world. The invaders are the ones overpopulating the world. Kill the invaders, kill the over-population and by doing so save the environment.' The shooter did not follow the recent move in overpopulation discourse from 'too little civilization' to 'too much': this is not an overpopulation argument considering the environmental impact of actual resource use (which would be substantially more for rich Westerners than most others), but one concerned with the absolute numbers of those the far right considers 'invaders'. Later in the manifesto, immigration is equated with environmental warfare. In a section entitled 'Green Nationalism Is the Only True Nationalism', he writes, alongside an assertion of the intimate connections between land and people: 'continued immigration into Europe is environmental warfare and ultimately destructive to nature itself'.

These intimate connections between land and people and the fixation on the destruction that immigration entails are conflated with climate change. In response to the question 'Why focus on immigration and birth rates when climate change is such a huge issue?', he writes 'Because they are the same issue', before returning to his theme of overpopulation.

Climate change and 'replacement' are also unified through their shared sense of catastrophic non-localizable crisis. Both require an immediate response: in response to a self-posed question, 'Why attack immigrants when "x" are the issue?', he writes, 'Because the "x" groups can be dealt with in time, but the high fertility immigrants will destroy us now, soon it is a matter of survival we destroy them first.' Urgency is everything in dealing with immigration. This sense of inexorable catastrophe – which originates from a fear of 'demographic decline' – can be grafted onto climate breakdown. Like 'degeneracy', 'environmental degradation' (in the nebulous way it is understood on the far right) can be read into more or less anything even slightly unusual. It is this process of grafting – moving from 'demographic decline' to climate change – that produces some of the complex motives of far-right terrorism.

Such a temporality of decline is familiar on the far right. That the contemporary world is 'fallen' and that social progress in the liberal sense condemns us to ever-greater moral degeneracy are axiomatic ideas on large sections of the far right. For many on the far right this sense of inexorable decline can only be arrested by the most radical social change: total social revolution. But for the blackpilled, even this possibility is blocked off. Social revolution of whatever kind, even if it were possible (and the blackpilled believe it is not), would not alter the facts of the matter. We are already substantially 'locked in', committed to what our past actions have bequeathed us in terms of atmospheric carbon levels, and in terms of replacement. (Again, generational blame is conferred on those who came before, as it is for the current demographic makeup of society.) No revolution of the spirit or the *Volk*, no matter how determined, will undo this. Thus, the most radical conclusion: the only possible response is cleansing violence.

The Base

The historian Roger Griffin, best known for his work on fascism, splits terrorism into 'two very distinct ... relationships to modernization ... one which seeks to ward off the culture-cidal threat [modernization] poses to an existing cultural tradition, and another which seeks to transform a particular aspect of existing modernity or even create an entirely new society'.[5] While the first project is clearly visible in the two shootings discussed above, the attempt to create an entirely new society is less so. This does not mean that these groups can't articulate a future. But the future that they do articulate, as we discussed in *Post-Internet Far Right*, is one defined almost entirely by violence and crises.

It is precisely the fact that the 'system' (a concept whose very generality, like 'degeneracy' or 'environmental degradation' allows for a strangely selective fanaticism) can still experience such crises excites some sections of the far right. For those who urge 'system collapse', like the neo-Nazi group Atomwaffen, the crises of modernity are glimmers of hope. But collapse is not just the opportunity to assert power; it is also, as the apocalypse has often been understood, the coming of 'justice'. Modernity is shattered and the space for a new society is opened up. Violence on the far right, then, springs from two conceptions of political, cultural, societal or even demographic collapse: a rear-guard action to ward off collapse versus an opportunistic strike to bring about collapse.

Some groups, such as the international network The Base, combine both. They subscribe to 'accelerationism', an ideology that attempts not only to prepare for but also to instigate 'system collapse'. In doing so, they draw in recruits from prepping communities. Prepping cultures have long been part of the far-right worldview: the magazine *The Survivor* was founded by Kurt Saxon, a former member of the American Nazi Party. Much as the construction of the southern border wall can be read as an environmental adaptation policy for Trump, the wider turn towards prepping culture is the climate-collapse readiness politics of the blackpilled.

Alexandra Stern has analysed the use of the 'bioregion' in far-right politics, a scale between those of the ethnovillage and the globe: small enough to project dreams of total control onto, large enough not to be simply buffeted about by global crises.[6] Control of such a space is not only a question of politics, but related to an aesthetic of nature, and nature's connection to whiteness. Such an arcadian project is visible in the Northwest Front, which sought to transform the six most northwesterly states of the US into a whites-only ethnostate. Their programme, centred around family farms, seeks to provide 'social, racial, and environmental stability . . . for man in close rapport with Nature'.[7] This vision necessitated extreme violence. Harold Covington, the leader of the Northwest Front, penned novels on the path to such a future, which amount often to leafier versions of the neo-Nazi race war fantasy *The Turner Diaries*. Greg Johnson, a 'moderate' voice on the issue, rejects Covington's 'revolutionary fantasy literature' and instead calls for 'a well-planned, orderly, and humane process of ethnic cleansing'.[8] Nor are the bioregional ambitions of the Northwest Front aberrations from the state forms of settler-colonial power in the region. Until 1926 the state of Oregon had on its books laws excluding black people from living in the state.

The Base launched a few months after Covington died in July 2018. It described itself as 'an informal non-membership prepping network focused on globally imparting post-societal collapse guerrilla warfare knowledge, skills, training and bushcraft'.[9] Its leader, Rinaldo Nazzaro, operating under the pseudonym 'Norman Spear', articulated a connection between primitivism and fascism: 'Take the anarcho-primitivist idea of just living in the woods ... you would end up with National Socialist society. ... National Socialism's purpose was to forge a human society that was working in sync with the principles of nature.'[10] Images of landscapes saturate these fantasies. The deep green forests and mountains of the northwest US, with their characteristic Douglas firs, function not only as exemplars of 'white' landscapes but as landscapes ideal for guerrilla warfare. Some of The Base's most spectacular actions such as the arson of a mink farm in Sweden are not entirely out of keeping with the aims of other animal rights activism,[11] although their other actions and their specific methods in this case would place them far from the actions of this determinedly non-lethal movement.

Nazzaro – in a conceptual move typical on the far right which frames racial hierarchies as both naturalized *and* requiring continual violent reinforcement – argues that any separatist movement must be combined with guerrilla warfare: 'at some point someone's going to have to get their hands dirty ... whatever it is, lone wolves or formalized or whatever, in place on the ground, to force the change, and force the enemy to the negotiation table'.[12] This approach 'is ideal for separatist insurgency'.[13] The Base was a more or less explicit attempt to scale White Nationalist groups up to the level of an insurgency.

This turn towards extreme violence is perhaps the consequence of one further influence we might read into Nazzaro: Dylann Roof, who murdered nine African Americans in the Charleston church shooting. In writings found online, Roof criticized the Northwest Front for promoting an idea that 'just parralells [sic] the concept of White people running to the suburbs'.[14] Arguably, The Base is the consequence of an attempt to address this criticism.

Nazzaro speaks with some credibility on guerrilla warfare. In 2014 he 'worked with Special Operations Command (SOCOM), one of the most secretive elements of the U.S. military and the tip of the spear in the war against jihadist terror groups like ISIS and al-Qaeda'.[15] The company Nazzaro led had a Commercial and Government Entity (CAGE) code, required to become a supplier for the US Department of Defense.[16] This revelation triggered a wave of uncertainty amongst The Base members and ridicule amongst the wider far right, bolstering claims that The Base was a honeypot. However, this was not all: Nazzaro was also living in central St Petersburg,[17] triggering suggestions the group was a Russian-funded fifth-columnist organization using anti-state militia movements in the US to destabilize the US government.[18] So, to summarize, a blur of masks: neo-Nazi, separatist, prepper, militia, FBI and perhaps some Russian state agency. What allows this wild syncretism?

Each of these political forms opposes itself absolutely to softness. These movements attempt to carve out a distinct space of control from a situation *they presume is hostile*. In each, a particular kind of self-reliance and resistance to comfort becomes the mark of masculinity: against the seductions of modern society, the security the state affords and the space owned by someone else, they oppose the pariah status, the ever-vigilant stance, the discomfort of contact with danger, and even the pleasure of fearing the worst.

More radically than just affirmations of scarcity, these movements are all affirmations of privation. Their adherents weaponize themselves as fully as possible, seemingly driving towards a natural principle of intensification for its own sake. Such an intensification for the sake of intensification explains why, despite Nazzaro's public strategizing, the movement itself seems to have resisted the imposition of this strategy. In 2020 three members were arrested on their way to a gun rally in Virginia where, according to FBI documents, they were planning to start violence enough to trigger a race war.[19]

Nazzaro's connections to the military are not unusual on the far right: it is possible to track waves of the far right in the US reasonably closely to waves of veterans returning from war.[20] We might suggest there are other connections. Contemporary warfare is clearly racialized: Muslims in the Middle East are understood as more 'killable' than white people. And yet, the actions of those recruits who wish to take advantage of this killability are nevertheless constrained by both the legal apparatus, however inconsistently applied, of international rules of engagement, and by the vast logistical apparatus of contemporary militaries themselves. What far-right racists in the military seem to believe *should* be a manifestation of their naturalized superiority turns out instead to depend on vast, alienating systems of command and control that ultimately seems to constrain the exercise of their power, even as it affords it. The Base and other ruralist military fantasy organizations seek to overcome these constraints. Both the method – guerrilla warfare – and the ultimate end goal – realized racial autonomy – of The Base are bound up with the same fantasy of personal naturalized (and biologized) domination, free from the constraints of the law. The nature politics of these groups justifies the wielding of the naturalized power that has been obscured by modernity.

Ultimately, the FBI destroyed The Base. Other accelerationist groups were gone in a flash: The Green Brigade, launched in November 2019, rapidly accrued 1,000 followers on Telegram, where it described itself as 'an organization consisting of openly accelerationist, militant environmentalist members focused on tearing down the system that exploits our people, land and animals', before disbanding in March 2020.[21] The similarly short-lived Eco-Fascist Order produced some of the clearest forms of 'ecofascist' ideology. 'Fascism IS nature, and nature IS Fascism', declared a post on their website. As ever, how 'nature' is conceptualized matters. Here, the extracted characteristic is hierarchy. 'Most all of us agree that hierarchy's [sic] exist and are necessary, yet still reject the only worldview that depends on where hierarchy's [sic] came from in the first place!'[22] Others produced viler propaganda: the National Socialist Order, a reincarnation of

Atomwaffen Division, a group linked to multiple murders, counting some of its own members as victims, published materials criticizing experiments on animals and advocating using Jews as experimental 'animals' instead.[23]

Radical flank dynamics

There has been, since the Second World War, tension between terrorism and organized far-right movements. And yet there is also a 'radical flank' effect in social movements. In the case of the Civil Rights movement in America, it was the dynamic between the radical flank (represented most emblematically by Malcolm X) and the more moderate wing (Martin Luther King Jr) that made the movement so effective. The radical fringe could be blamed for the excesses of the movement and make the moderate wing's radicalism seem comparatively mild. What kinds of radical flank effects have been taking place for the right, both in the case of the Christchurch shooting and in the case of The Base?

If the far right's general strategy can be described as 'metapolitics', 'a war of social transformation, at the level of worldview, thought, and culture', in the words of one of its most active proponents, then deadly violence intervenes in the context of this strategy.[24] Metapolitics is not strictly opposed to mass shootings.[25] The fallout from them is complex. In the case of the Christchurch shooting, this attack invited condemnation from across the political spectrum, even as its political content was deliberately obscured. Kellyanne Conway, an important figure in the Trump administration, attempted to reframe the attack by appealing to the long history of the US Green Scare, as the work of an (implicitly left-wing) 'eco-terrorist'.[26] The opposite tack was seemingly taken by the BBC, who brought the pan-Europeanist far-right group Generation Identity, promoters of the Great Replacement conspiracy theory, onto the news to explain their beliefs. It later emerged that the Christchurch shooter had donated to Generation Identity before the attack. Despite this unopposed platforming of their ideology, Generation Identity are at the time of writing a subdued force, although this has less to do with the attack and more to do with preexisting legal troubles. Here, the shooting was arguably beneficial for Generation Identity and their metapolitical project. They became, if only momentarily, a well-known group, their politics broadcast widely.

In the case of The Base, regardless of whether it was a honeypot, it had that effect: many would-be terrorists were arrested, and the popularity of groups on the 'blackpilled' section of the far right waned. It would be excessive, however, to lay the broader decline of the US alt-right at the feet of either The Base or the El Paso shooting.

But perhaps the problem with the question of the radical flank is that it presupposes a far-right 'mainstream' that is opposed to violence. Other far-right movements, even those much closer to the mainstream of politics, do not consistently reject violence. Even if the radical flank of the blackpilled is the point of the greatest intensification towards violence, the mass conspiratorial movements spurred on by QAnon have built on previous waves of conspiratorial mass politics in the US such as the militia movement, the Tea Party and wider conspiracy culture to provide the basis for a violence carried out by those who would not consider themselves fringe. The participants in the riot at the US Capitol in January 2021 were not misanthropic violence-fixated people detached from society. Yet their action resulted in violent deaths amid calls to hang Vice-President Mike Pence. Nor is death in the contemporary climatic regime the exclusive preserve of terrorists or movements: thousands die every year at borders through the action or indifference of states, and millions from the slow violence of environmental degradation.

It is essential to keep in sight the contiguity between the terroristic parts of the far right and the other parts. We have already seen how the ideas of both the Christchurch and the El Paso shooters were not out of keeping with wider far-right overpopulation or anti-immigrant discourse. The ability of far-right organizations to accommodate extreme acts of violence will define their more general viability in the context of climate breakdown. Now, more than at any point since the Second World War, the question of violence hovers below the surface of the far right, a tendency that will only increase as we move into escalating climate systems breakdown.

5

Towards ecofascism proper?

Three futures

Let's look to the future. In *Dialectic of Enlightenment*, Theodor Adorno and Max Horkheimer write on 'the stupidity of cleverness': 'I recall a conversation [before the Second World War] with an economist who demonstrated the impossibility of Germany's militarization from the interests of Bavarian brewers ... Clever people have always made things easy for barbarians, because they are so stupid.'[1] Intricate arguments were and are constructed to prove fascism's impossibility. Let us assert now, then: fascism, or something very much like it, could happen again.

But there is also another risk: while expecting fascism, we forget the variety of authoritarian politics. Future forms of it might have little to do with interwar fascism. As Stuart Hall remarked on the left's struggle against neoliberalism, 'the simple slogans of "fascism" are more than useless here – they cover up, conveniently, everything which it is most important to keep in view'.[2]

Similarly, Eric Bonds writes that while 'ecofascism' 'may well be spectacular, [it] is scarcely the only form of risk.

Continuing as we are will impact the lives of hundreds of millions of people as food scarcity, heat death, pandemics, and other impacts of climate change escalate. At present, the lobbying of fossil fuel companies remains a more dangerous and destructive practice than the machinations of right-environmentalism.'[3] However, this is not quite right: the two are entirely compatible, as Andreas Malm and the Zetkin Collective have shown. The power of the fossil fuel companies, and the continuation of the climate crisis that comes from it, makes everything less stable, and so lays the groundwork for future far-right projects.[4]

Why might the far right gain from climate systems breakdown more than the left? The effects of this breakdown are likely to emerge as complex social crises. In the face of such crises, many people might adopt radical political parochialism. Nationalism, the various forms of racism, and other reactionary attachments might deepen in a more uncertain world, especially one with such stark geographical disparities and an increasing idea of nature as an antagonist. As Christian Parenti writes, 'There is a real risk that strong states with developed economies will succumb to a politics of xenophobia, racism, police repression, surveillance, and militarism and thus transform themselves into . . . neofascist islands of relative stability in a sea of chaos.'[5] This is what the historian Geoff Eley called 'gatedness as the emergent social paradigm'.[6]

In the last few chapters, we've seen the complexity, even chaos of far-right politics, and its relations to the ideas of nature and the politics of climate change. In speculating on its future, we simplify. But such exercises can also clarify how to disrupt such formations as they begin to assemble.

The nativist movement

Under climate change conditions, nativist movements are likely to emerge, attempting to 'hold on to remnants of the past by attempting to exclude or eliminate particular groups of people or ideas, beliefs, customs, and objects from a society'.[7] Who would constitute such a movement? Perhaps a whole complicated mess of groups: conspiracists, authoritarians, denialists, nostalgists, China-hawks and admirers, cultural reactionaries and racists, anti-migrant activists and so on.

The ideological convictions of such a nativist movement would be important, but fervent belief is insufficient for success. It would become, however, truly conflagratory if it lined up with substantial capital (or, in other words, business) interests. There are perhaps two fractions of capital that could give such a movement a place on the global stage. The movement might ally with either, such is the broad indeterminacy of current far-right nature politics.

The first project, 'Fossilized Reaction', is protective of fossil capital and willing to take denial and obfuscation as far as possible. It pushes for the militarization of society against all kinds of threats, and tries to maintain access to its spoils. The second, 'Batteries, Bombs and Borders', alloys climate change mitigation with the maintenance of Western hegemony (in a likely 'New Cold War' situation):[8] militarization abroad and intensifying, perhaps increasingly xenophobic, control of populations domestically and at its borders. We might think of it as an 'ecogovernance turn' within conventional imperial power, with an added green-tech-capital edge.

The central question of capitalist governance is: 'How will capital continue to be accumulated?' Both these potential futures are thus 'system loyal', they are both in favour of aspects of the existing property regime, namely those that benefit their corresponding slice of capital;[9] in the former, fossil fuels, in the latter, a combination of the security industries, green tech and, indeed, most of the rest of capital. Both futures attempt to defend (different segments) of property.

But not all the nativist movement's impulses will be capturable by one of these fractions. Such a movement might also spawn another far-right project, which we call

'Climate Collapse Cultists'. In this project, the idea of nature is used to justify killing, either by a more or less coherent movement, or by comparatively isolated actors. This 'project', unlikely to scale like the others, might nevertheless expand significantly beyond its current state, terrorizing its targets and pushing for ever-more radical racial politics in the other projects.

The danger of this last project and the first is clear: either sporadic deadly violence, or no action on climate change. But the second also represents a serious danger, not just because its attempts to mitigate climate change involve the maintenance and intensification of the current regimes of global governance (this time involving more renewable energy), but because, as an attempt to succeed at global superpower competition, it is unlikely to actually mitigate climate change significantly.

Let's go through these three – 'Fossilized Reaction', 'Batteries, Bombs and Borders' and 'Climate Collapse Cultists' – in some more detail.

'Fossilized Reaction'

There are trillions of dollars of oil reserves globally – reserves that, if they were to be extracted and burnt, would raise global temperatures to a point of global mass destruction. The material infrastructure of fossil fuels is already in place 'and the owners of those investments will invariably choose to recoup some of that investment rather than none of it'.[10] As rapidly as renewable technologies might come online, other new technologies in the mining sector have made viable forms of extraction of fossil fuels that were previously not,[11] such as shale oil, which, economically inefficient as it is, secures for the US the national security objective of temporary energy independence.[12] The first future we outline – 'Fossilized Reaction' – is the political wing of capital wholly committed, both ideologically and financially, to fossil fuel extraction. With its combination of fossil fuels, denialism and securitization, this future could be extrapolated from the current politics of Trump and Bolsonaro.

Nor can fossil fuels simply be replaced without pushback. Environmental movements attempting to dislodge fossil fuels have come to expect serious resistance. As Andreas Malm has written, the fossil fuel industry 'is not a sideshow to bourgeois democracy . . . it is the material form of contemporary capitalism'. Attempting to replace such a system is not akin to the struggle against 'a relic from an authoritarian age that requires correction' but against the '*productive forces* imbricated in certain property relations'.[13]

'Fossilized reaction' will eventually fall. But the damage and delay it could have plausibly caused by then would be immense, possibly terminal for society writ large. And it would fail to securitize its own position. As Christian Parenti tells it, crises of 'hunger, disease, criminality, fanaticism, and violent social breakdown – will overwhelm the armed lifeboat. Eventually, all will sink into the same morass'.[14]

'Batteries, Bombs and Borders'

The second future – 'Batteries, Bombs and Borders' – is orientated towards mitigation, but deepens global inequities in pursuit of it. Green energy technologies (solar panels, lithium batteries, wind turbines and so on) cannot be conjured out of the air. They require – among other preconditions – the command of non-renewable rare earth minerals, which might in the future take on a status not dissimilar from oil now – with all the geopolitical strife that entails.[15] More generally, 'in the fourth machine age, access to raw materials continues to be systematically secured by extraeconomic means . . . police trucks, water cannons, surveillance cameras, tear gas, and barbed wire'.[16] In this future, the military plays an extremely important role in both mitigation (securing global supplies of necessary minerals) and in adaptation (securitizing US society against climate change's worst effects).

In this future, nature politics is one ideological battle-ground of a new China–US Cold War. Some on the far right, like Steve Bannon, have long portrayed China as a threat to Western civilization. But, as we discussed earlier, for some, China also serves as a model of effective coercion of the kind that more democratic states can only dream of.[17] For this future, China's form of authoritarian environmentalism, presented as the only viable way to save humanity, might start to look more attractive. Accepting the reality of climate change is clearly compatible with authoritarian politics: especially if the securitization of existing political infrastructure can be presented as essential to preserving the environment itself.

Because of its sheer scale, fighting climate change trumps all else. To avert the worst effects, almost anything might seem proportionate. For this reason, arguments against this future must be phrased not as arguments of decency, but to point to the counterproductiveness that lies in the requirement for extensive militarization, armies being some of the most carbon-intensive entities in the world.

Such a 'New Cold War' will be full of disputes over the geopolitics of renewable energy and mutual blame for ecological destruction. It relies for its appeal on the understanding of renewable energy technologies as free from 'negative externalities' and, what's more, virtuous. There is a danger that the deployment of green (and its close synonym, 'clean') technologies will obscure its concomitant production of extractive 'sacrifice zones', which frequently seem to require authoritarian violence to enforce and maintain.[18]

A recent moment that exemplifies this future best is probably the 2019 coup in Bolivia, widely considered to have been related to the country's lithium resources.[19] Here, the far-right movement in question was not in the Global North, but in Bolivia itself. Such acts have a long history – the use of far-right politics to impose market 'liberalization' is a long-running tendency in the history of Latin America in particular. Perhaps in the future it will have a green justification. Although he wasn't involved, Elon Musk, CEO of Tesla (which relies on lithium supplies), tweeted in the aftermath of the coup: 'We'll coup whoever we want! Deal with it'.[20] Bolivia's president hinted in March 2021 that he believed Tesla was involved.[21]

In this future, the far right will use the imperative of restricting emissions to argue for the necessity of halting immigration entirely. The argument need not have changed much from its past deployments: more people in richer countries means more emissions. And, again, it would miss the most important dimension of environmental impact, which is wealth and not race.

Migration might also not have the rationale it had for the bourgeoisie in the past. On the one hand, an ageing workforce requires more migration to replace it, and on the other, the challenge of automation decreases the economic need for migration into large countries.[22] The balance of the two sets the stage for future migration politics. The transformation of Danish politics since the Global Financial Crisis is a useful lesson in the possible suddenness of the transformation: there, the centre left and the far right rapidly converged around anti-migration politics.[23]

This future and the 'Fossilized Reaction' one are engaged in a hellish cycle of producing and responding to migration: migration on the southern US border is arguably traceable back to a century of US interference in the politics of the home countries of migrants, destabilizing countries and rendering them incapable of solving their own problems. Migration follows, to which the more reactionary elements of the right respond by intensifying border regimes and agitating popular racist sentiments.

This is a tragic future: in dealing with climate change simply as a problem of atmospheric gas (although it is, of course, also that), and not as a more complex social problem of living well in a volatile world, this future can at once seem to address the problem, and intensify the suffering it entails.

Because of its comparatively clear-eyed acceptance of much of the science around climate change, this 'Batteries, Bombs and Borders' future might appear as an inflection within existing environmental movements, i.e. as the resolution of an apparent contradiction between accepting immigration to the Global North and rapidly reducing production and consumption in those countries. However, we should be clear that in its perpetuation and intensification of global inequality, it is far from an ally of the left.

All viable futures, such as those proposed by the Green New Deal, need extractive processes to be ramped up to produce renewable energy. Mining *is* destructive, but it need not be catastrophic or so profoundly inequitable. It is the danger of this 'Batteries, Bombs and Borders' future that means that supporters of the Green New Deal must maintain their commitments also to climate justice.

Conventional post-Cold War far-right talking points are bolstered by appeals to the climate crisis: 'we must halt immigration because it dilutes our culture' becomes stronger because migration can be presented as entailing further climate systems breakdown. In the terms of either project, it might be claimed 'the world has fundamentally departed from the natural order of things; we must set it right'. But the strongest version of this nature politics comes in the third project – 'Climate Collapse Cults'.

'Climate Collapse Cults'

This project revolves around deadly violence. Such a project represents the return of a logic of killing to the comparatively organized parts of the far right (although we should of course note that 'organized' is likely to mean something very different in a world thoroughly remade by the internet). The electoral far right has long disavowed the more radical fringe. But this need not always be the case.

'Climate Collapse Cults' responds to the escalation of crises by attempting to intensify the two terroristic movements we mapped on the fringes of the right: on the one hand, the murderous attempt to either halt modernity or to isolate oneself from it, and in doing so, create a new world. The more degraded the world becomes through climate change, perhaps the more far-right terrorists will attempt a synthesis of the two. Ambivalence about modernity has often been at the core of far-right politics; it simply gains its clearest expression in terrorism.

Others have written of the danger of 'bioconservative' terrorism, 'an ideology that is belligerent and even hostile towards technological optimism'.[24] Existent groups, like the Mexican Individualists Tending to the Wild (Individualistas Tendiendo a lo Salvaje, ITS), promote anti-tech radicalism and portray the indiscriminateness of their violence as evidence of their integrity with nature.[25] It is not difficult to see how such a project, like other supposedly nihilistic tendencies (the early-2000s imageboard culture which hybridized with other seemingly unrelated currents to form the alt-right, for example), might discover an underlying reactionary core beneath its supposed rejection of all values.[26] However, such a movement would be highly unpredictable, perhaps blending ideologies into dense syncretic amalgams, almost impossible to predict, and responding flexibly to crises.

Crises of governance

Christian Parenti writes: 'Climate change arrives in a world primed for crisis. The current and impending dislocations of climate change intersect with the already-existing crises of poverty and violence ... problems compound and amplify each other, one expressing itself through another.'[27] Parenti's conception of a 'catastrophic convergence' allows us to see that climate change is neither distinct from existing structures nor simply a slight generalized intensification of existing crises but intersects with other crises in cascading feedback loops.

Far-right politics has historically relied on crises to scale. Its power relies on a sense that radical action is immediately required. Such a sense of crisis can, of course, be manufactured. Yet not all crises benefit the right. We must therefore be more specific. What will happen in the next 50 years of climate breakdown?

Here, we look at migration crises, pandemics, economic crises and wars, as well as transformations in our collective capacity to know. Each problem throws up its own variant of governance in response. But because the problems overlap and 'express themselves through each other', they might seem to require a form of *total governance*, the temptation of authoritarian expansion.[28] It is largely within this authoritarian expansion that the far right will situate their responses to the complex sum of these problems, each perhaps superficially revolutionary. Indeed, without reducing our opposition to its ideas one bit, we might nevertheless admit that, as they have in the past, the far right might once again offer 'plausible solutions to modern social problems'.[29] There is likewise no particularly good reason to imagine that future far-right politics will be inflexible or hopeless. But there is plenty of good reason to believe it will be disastrous.

How might the three far-right projects above engage this convergence of crises? More generally, will authoritarian and reactionary variants of capitalism out-compete its liberal varieties in the context of climate change? Or, as two moments of a geographically differentiated regime of governance, aren't liberalism and authoritarianism perfectly compatible anyway?

Or, how might the escalating scale of governance crises under neoliberalism itself produce the conditions for authoritarianism? In his book *Disaster Capitalism*, Antony Loewenstein widens Naomi Klein's argument that capital uses disasters to expand its reach into life. Fractions of capital create problems in anticipation of providing their solutions.[30] In a different register, crises form the basis for 'securitization' moves. The failure to address a problem becomes an opportunity for a more securitized and profitable response. These failures are, as Nicholas Beuret has argued, constitutive parts of neoliberal governance.[31] We might even say that mitigating and capitalizing on risks are opposed more generally. It is these constitutive failures of governance, and not the crises themselves, that open the door to authoritarianism and the politics of the far right. A case in point, the European migration crisis of 2015, which precipitated a substantial uptick in the power of far-right parties in Europe, was not a crisis because of the number of migrants, but a consequence of consistent failures of European governments to adequately fund the required humanitarian response.

But another danger here, in addition to the expansion of neoliberalism, is that such responses are 'contrary to neoliberal political rationalities',[32] and, moreover, democratic ones. When crises expand, neoliberal strategies of 'containment' and failure become entirely inadequate. The scale is simply too big: 'faced with the catastrophic problem of climate change, failure [and subsequent securitizing moves] no longer holds utility as a means of governance'.[33] But such authoritarian expansions are far from the necessary consequence of crisis. Each crisis need not been understood as an existential struggle between racially distinct groups for naturally scarce resources.

The crises that climate change produces can be analysed separately, but there are nevertheless hugely complex consequences to each. By early August 2010, it was clear that the harvest yields all over Russia had declined sharply. The country, which had produced more wheat than it consumed since 2004, had entered a period of drought over the summer, and had banned wheat exports in response.[34] The 2010 Russian crop failure led to an increase in the price of grain. This sent food prices spiralling across North Africa and the Middle East, and (some have argued) triggered the movements of the Arab Spring and its subsequent authoritarian crackdown, most prominently in Syria, from which millions of people were forced to flee. Many – although by no means all – entered Europe. The far right gained hugely in elections shortly after.[35] None of this is to suggest a direct or simple causality between these events: indeed, the point of the example is precisely to emphasize the cascading complexity of seemingly unrelated events in a fragile and interconnected world. Such run-on events are inevitable, but the responses to them are not.

The far right has profited from perceived crises of migration for over a century. It was a period of large-scale migration into North America that gave fuel to the fire of Grantian nativist politics before and after the First World War. The National Front in the UK was boosted by vitriolic hatred against immigrants from South Asia in the 1970s and 1980s. During the 2010s, the failure of European management of migration into Europe boosted the fortunes of the European far right, prominent among them the pan-Europeanist Generation Identity.

Generation Identity organized the Defend Europa campaign, which crowdfunded a boat to 'patrol the Mediterranean' to push back migrants attempting the dangerous crossing into Europe. This made a spectacle of order at the contemporary state's maximum point of fragility, the border. Where the state in the early twentieth century appeared weak because of its lack of control of the metropolis (to which fascists responded by marching through the cities), the state in the early twenty-first century appears weak because it apparently does not control its borders (the actual massive accretion of border technologies notwithstanding).

This is why migration politics, although not a major part of the state's total activities, is so important for far-right movements which contest the power of the state: it is at once at the edges, where the state of exception always seems possible, and directly in the centre of democratic governance, in that it controls the construction of the population itself. Further, under neoliberalism, capital's need for cheap labour mixes with the collective social insecurity that neoliberalism produces to prompt the far right's anti-immigrant response. Neoliberalism's dependency on cheapened racialized labour lays the groundwork for the flourishing of racist anti-migration politics.[36]

In the long term, the declining population in Europe will mean that, from the perspective of neoliberal governance, it might be entirely rational to increase immigration. That means that the far right is likely to stand in quite sharp relief to central organizational strategies of neoliberal climate politics. However, the possible (automation-dependent) capitalist necessity of large-scale immigration into Europe, the US and other wealthy countries is not an argument against the possibility of far-right politics scaling, but only sets the stage for a more sharply defined showdown between neoliberalism and the far right. This showdown, to the extent that neoliberal crisis management continues to respond to migration with securitizing moves, will continue to benefit the far right.

Climate change is also likely to make pandemics more frequent. Faced with the COVID-19 pandemic, the right-populists in power acted sluggishly. In the UK and US, responses were marred by decades of declining state capacity and marked by glib pronouncements, uneven lockdowns and confused messaging. Bolsonaro's government in Brazil spread denial and campaigned against lockdowns, as did Trump. The right wing of neoliberal governance opted for dithering negligence. The initial failure to act in any clear way might have seemed peculiar, and it is this failure – insisting that the function of government remains, in the words of Joshua Clover to '*make work and let buy*' – that opens up space for the far right.[37]

Some on the far right argued that lockdown measures should have happened sooner, a view shared by many groups across the political spectrum. They also drew the evergreen conclusion that the spread of the virus proved the validity of their go-to policy: 'ending globalism'.[38] Others on the far right indulged in conspiracies and eyed the anti-lockdown movements as a potential base of support. It is the dynamic between these two modes of governance: on the one hand, calls for strict authoritarian control, and on the other, conspiratorial chaos, which will likely define future far-right politics. The pandemic, although it seemed to undermine those parts of the far right still mostly committed to neoliberalism, benefited the wider, more heterogeneous forces to their right, less loyal to the existing order.

The argument made in the 2015 migration crisis – that some refugees were terrorists – was modified in 2020 at the beginning of the pandemic. It was instead suggested that the migrants were infected with COVID-19, and migration thus became a question of public health. Here, entirely reasonable measures for the maintenance of public health dovetail – tragically – with the arguments of the far right. Perhaps we should be happy therefore that, when faced with this wide opening for the application of their politics, the far right largely acted in a manner more conspiratorial than authoritarian, mainly ditching their calls for harsher measures in favour of declarations that the whole thing was a hoax.

What effects might financial crises have? The Great Depression provided a vital boost to the Nazi party's electoral ambitions. Increases in support for the Nazis were concentrated in towns with Danatbank branches, the bank at the centre of the collapse in Germany. The crisis also provided an opportunity to Nazi propagandists, who singled out Danat's Jewish chairman for blame and more generally 'blamed economic misery on Jewish "high finance"'.[39] Similarly, the Great Recession has perhaps been more significant than anything else in accelerating the rise of the far right in recent years.

Financial crises are likely to become more frequent under climate change conditions, not least because financial crises are indicators of transformations in systemic risk conditions.[40] In the immediate wake of the pandemic, Aaron Benanav anticipated a labour market slower to recover than the Great Financial Crisis that preceded it, which itself was a historically slow recovery. As we expect slower and less substantial recoveries, we should also expect the expansion of precarious work and income insecurity.[41] There is a danger that, as before, ongoing unemployment, precariousness and destitution creates populations amenable to the appeals of the far right. However, the solution of the Great Recession, as Dylan Riley has argued, came through the expansion of debt which produced the social conditions of atomization. This atomization, as we have suggested, is perhaps not conducive to fascism, although it was clearly useful to other forms of the far right.[42]

Historical fascism built itself on war. The future – whatever the effectiveness of climate mitigation – will have *some* form of war. If mitigation is unsuccessful, then the world will become radically more unsafe. However, even with mitigation, recent research has suggested that the geopolitics of renewable energy is likely to produce many more small wars.[43] Such a tendency is supplemented with the tendency towards 'new wars'. These wars, Mary Kaldor argues, are characterized by 'heavy civilian casualties, crime networks, blurry lines of enmity, complex humanitarian crises, and indiscernibly civil and internationalized participants'. Such complex problems have formed the basis for much of the far right's discussion of migration in the US: drug cartels in Central America are one of the most common reasons given to clamp down on migration. The transformation of 'war' into 'security' and the 'collapse of the distinctions between combat and policing'[44] drive the production of these 'new wars'. Other transformations in war are also underway: recent conflicts have been cyber-dominated[45] but in the future, direct command of ecosystems themselves is likely to become a more explicit aspect of warfare.[46]

As we have noted before, far-right movements, at least in the US, are correlated with the return of veterans from wars,[47] and, moreover, an increase in the forms of terroristic violence discussed above. In the case of the far right, we might suggest that this interlinking between environmental change and violent extremism will only escalate, and in turn feed back on itself. The nativist movement demands securitization, which produces wars, which produce veterans, who radicalize the movement.[48] Parenti summarizes the 'essence of militarized adaptation to climate chaos: dirty war forever'.[49] This logic of killing might have quite another structure in countries first hit by the worst of climate change: 'In some resource-poor fragile states, nonstate armed groups will fill the void left by the state, providing basic services to gain the trust and support of the local population.'[50]

However, it is important to note that research into the linkage of climate change to conflict is, in fact, inconclusive. Ben Hayes reports that 'a majority of scholars argue that governance and policy failure are, and will remain, far more important drivers of conflict than climate change'.[51] There is a danger of depoliticizing violence, shearing it of its history, and turning towards climate reductionism, in which violence in the Global South is naturalized as a feature of the climate itself, or as a direct feature of the people, bound to that climate, as we discussed it had been a prominent argument in colonialism.[52]

Similarly, wars over scarce resources, often thought of through the prism of 'securitization', are not a necessary consequence of the renewable energy transition. Phillipe Le Billon argues that the contingency of resources wars as a form must be emphasized. 'Popular (geo)political narratives of resource wars have mostly drawn on Hobbesian and neo-Malthusian perspectives; in essence perspectives that assert violent (but rational) scrambles over scarce and valuable resources', and should be rejected.[53] In terms of the three futures outlined above, none is likely to shy away from war, although their characters are likely to be very different. In the case of 'Batteries, Bombs and Borders', such wars might even have perverse and unpredictable incentives: no longer securing oil but rare earth minerals for a renewable energy transition.

In finding support for such wars, the changing character of far-right movements is of great importance. Much of the independent far right in the US has historically been opposed to US interventionism abroad and fearful of encroaching state power domestically. In the Trump period, this partially changed. The QAnon conspiracy theory has enabled a shift away from such conspiracies towards support for the behind-the-scenes machinations of 'military intelligence'.

Far-right ecologism and its future

Throughout this book, we have identified many different components of a far-right ideology of nature. We summarize them here so as to speculate on their future. Far-right ecologism associates particular animals with particular races; asserts a deep and unique connection between whiteness and nature; and more generally expresses an obsession with racial purity as indicative of a 'natural order'. It displaces blame for environmental destruction onto racialized others, expressed often through a pathological attempt to distinguish the dirty from the clean as well as its promulgation of neo-Malthusian population thinking. Even more extremely, it places outside this racialized nature Jews, who are imagined as perverters or derangers of nature's law.

It imagines a temporality in which the world is moved ever further from nature's regulatory ideals and towards degeneracy, often imagined as the apparent influence of Jews. This tendency towards degeneracy culminates in an apocalyptic image of the end of the world. To forestall this, it expresses its desire to return to *völkisch* simplicity, a desire often in tension with its modernizing aspects, which include, at the most extreme end, a desire for genocide. Sometimes this genocidal hatred is justified by an extremely crude version of Social Darwinism built around selection without variation and sometimes also by appeal to the 'natural law' that 'might is right'.

Each of these aspects of far-right ecologism is well established. And yet, climate change adds further complexities still: it transforms and intensifies these old aspects and creates new ones. Its future transformations will come in the context of a wider crisis of knowability that will disrupt the utility of science and open the door for a deepening of conspiratorial thinking.

Some have argued for a bleak conclusion: we have probably reached peak predictive knowledge of the natural world. As climate change makes the world more volatile, patterns which might become more opaque to us in the near future include 'the prevalence of crop and human pests, like locust plagues set off by drought conditions; forest fire frequency; the dynamics of the predator-prey food chain; . . . and the predictability of agricultural output'. These are largely medium-term patterns: between a month and a decade. 'As Earth warms, our historical understanding will turn obsolete faster than we can replace it with new knowledge.' The power of our predictive modelling is decreasing.[54]

With weaker predictive power, we face what William Gail, former President of the American Meteorological Society, calls a 'New Dark Age'. This opens the door to conspiracy theorists, one of the characteristic modes of far-right politics. The common story of the last ten years – the splintering of the public sphere and the rise of 'fake news' – is supplemented in the case of complex climate events by a genuine form of uncertainty. Science, once so seemingly in command of the world, might increasingly seem to be nothing better than a set of guesses, vulnerable to sudden and spectacular delegitimization by moments of popular conspiratorial deflation.

Conspiracy theorizing seeks to find single pieces of conclusively falsifying evidence. As the texture of a given crisis changes, even in quite mundane ways, these changes are taken as evidence that the crisis itself is unreal. For example, in the COVID-19 pandemic, as hospitals filled up, the received image of what a 'hospital stretched to breaking pointing' *should* look like was undercut. Images of empty corridors were taken as evidence that the pandemic was unreal, ignoring that the *specifics* of this novel crisis required precisely this. What was in truth evidence of the crisis was taken as evidence of its unreality, because our images of past crises were suddenly inadequate (perhaps, in this example, footage of bustling hospitals in the aftermath of a terrorist attack).

This is not quite the same as the climate denialism discussed in previous chapters. It accepts that *something has changed*. Those who said that the COVID-19 pandemic was fake rarely thought that everything was fine. They understood that there was a crisis, but disagreed about what had happened. Such beliefs are not the brittle assertion that change is fundamentally impossible. Instead, they consist in a supple sense that because things are not as they seem, then any other form of explanation becomes permissible. It is almost impossible to overstate this capacity for the transformation of conspiracies. In early 2021, after Joe Biden had been sworn in as US President, portions of the QAnon conspiracy movement, who had been expecting Biden and the 'deep state' to be arrested at the inauguration, pivoted to the belief that Biden himself *was Trump*, or possibly was a clone, or possibly there simply had been no inauguration at all, and thus the intricate plan to bring the 'deep state' to justice was still in motion.

What conspiracies in the future are likely to do is not *deny* climate change. Instead, they might instead make it fundamentally *unthinkable*. The past obfuscations of climate denialism will provide a rich resource for the production of future, weirder and less controllable conspiracies. Having been played with for so long by climate-denying groups, both on the far right and amongst the holders of fossil capital, what was before denial politics will form a kind of basis for the new conspiratorial politics. One of the central struggles of the twenty-first century will be to articulate a political aesthetics of disaster.

The rising difficulty science faces in predicting the world is supplemented by other epistemic challenges, also fruitful to conspiracy culture. What is a 'climate-related crisis event' anyway? The boundaries are, of course, hugely unclear: the climate is a factor in more or less anything, and in the current scholarly environment, the attribution of climate change as a prominent factor for an event carries with it an entire way of seeing the world. Climate change is, like all other 'hyperobjects', visible through its 'imprint on other things'.[55] Such a complex sense of causality, where 'phenomena of radically different dimensions' are integrated, might even be what 'makes modern climate science modern',[56] and yet it stands almost exactly opposed to the conspiratorial mindset, thirsty for clear demarcations of phenomena, even as it bends their explanations beyond credulity. Perhaps the central aesthetic experience of the twenty-first century will be derealization.

There is rising awareness of *systematic unintended consequences* (of which the rise in atmospheric carbon is the paradigmatic case). As Sverker Sörlin and Nina Wormbs write, 'the emerging *Weltanschauung* [worldview] [of nature in the climate crisis] is marked by the insight that human intervention in the world is no longer limited to the intentional. On the contrary, we increasingly discover that some of the most profound consequences of human actions are at the same time unintended and also comprehensive.'[57] Not only are we *not* at the centre of the world, but we are again subject (albeit unevenly) to more-than-human nature's immense powers, and the accidental effects of capitalism's own attempts at mastering it. Yet, for the conspiracy theorist, such complex causality is forbidden. Intentionality is all. Many kinds of reactionary thought have consistently attempted to resist such 'Copernican' turns and to re-centre humans, or some group of them.

There are two very different stories about technology in the twenty-first century. On the one hand, there is techno-optimism: Moore's law, terraforming, freely available green energy, kelp farming, bespoke algae production, space mining. The other, a much more sobering account, points to the dwindling resource base for these technologies as well as the deep inequalities that they reinforce.

The future, whatever else it might be, will be a future of deeply uneven temporalities. Privatized space exploration for some, slums the size of cities for others. Not one middle class, but many, spread from Lyon to Lanzhou, Lahore to Lagos and London to Lima. Gene editing technologies that can banish diseases and grow artificial meat in times of food crises and public health emergencies. Heat death, designer productivity drugs, ubiquitous algorithmic governance and barbed wire.

Far-right politics engages science and the fruits of modernization in an opportunistic manner. For example, the contemporary far right's conception of race overlays mythicized history with opportunistically selected aspects of 'race science'. While ancestry testing abstracts identity from history and places it instead in the individual's body (often indicating in the process a much more complicated personal history than the individual was expecting), it is not simply an individualizing move. Attempts on the far right to distil from the statistical complexities of genetic testing distinct races is dangerously misguided on two fronts: erroneous, even dishonest, analysis tied to a biologically essentializing conception of collective identity compatible both with historical fascism's obsessive attempts to categorize and further coercive biosecurity policies.

We can't yet answer with any certainty questions like: 'What would the far-right position on geoengineering be?' Although we might find examples of comparatively grand projects within the architecture of interwar fascism, geoengineering touches more profoundly on the question of human's relation to the environment. Nature politics takes a particularly intense turn around the subjects of genetic and geoengineering, where future technoscience is likely to make its most conspicuous and seemingly worrying innovations, worrying most strongly because they seem to transform the concept of nature itself.

Fascism, again?

Do we need the term 'fascism' for any of this? Let us restate our definition from earlier: Fascism is a political form that seeks to revolutionize and reharmonize the nation state through expelling a radically separate 'Other' by paramilitary means.

Many forms of domination, many forms of extreme violence, have not been fascism. 'Fascism' was not required for a host of oppressive, authoritarian actions carried out by non-fascist states over the course of the twentieth and twenty-first centuries. And all that has happened since the end of the Second World War seems to put a gap between us and the period of interwar fascism: wars of national liberation; feminism's second and third waves; the Cold War and its end; the collapse of social democracy and the rise of neoliberalism; the dissolving of many past forms of mass associationism; the invention of the internet; the establishment of a world market and the provincialization of Europe; automation; the rise of political Islam; and the rise of China. None of these events decisively eliminates the possibility of fascism, but they all mean that, if it returns, it will have a different character from last time.

Given all these distancing events, let us make the strongest possible case for what we have called 'Fossilized Reaction' as a form of fascism. To ramp up its exclusionary policies, it would need to secure the support of a broad section of the populace, against the demands of a radicalized environmental movement for the current regime of fossil capital to be dismantled. At first, it wouldn't necessarily require for its stabilization the paramilitarism Michael Mann argues is so important to fascism.[58] In the period since the Second World War the state has massively expanded its monopoly on violence. But this is only *at first*. The failure to mitigate climate change substantially can only lead to an escalating series of problems, necessitating the repression of movements against the dominant property regime, a process of escalation which might seemingly continue without end.

Nevertheless, this escalation of violence won't necessarily exist in the conditions stipulated by Dylan Riley's theory of fascism: mass associationism without hegemonic politics. Commenting on Trumpism, often claimed as a variant of fascism, Riley notes that it and 'its various European correlates have arisen, in contrast, in the context of a fragmented and depoliticized civil society'.[59] Neoliberalism's shredding of associational social forms has withered this aspect of the preconditions for fascism: people are just too isolated now. We can expect such a fragmentation process to continue in the short term, although some forms of mass associationism (notably conspiracy movements) are on the increase, as will be environmental movements in the near future, although that's far from being a fully realized return. This means it would exist in the context of a great number of projects competing for hegemony, Riley's other enabling condition for fascism. In short, the capacity of 'Fossilized Reaction' to turn into fascism depends on how bad climate change gets, the degree to which future environmental and conspiratorial politics becomes mass phenomena and the degree to which current hegemonic forms lose their traction. All three of these conditions are plausibly set towards the re-emergence of fascism.

Might 'Batteries, Bombs and Borders' also metastasize into a form of fascism? It no doubt expands the regime of violence and appeals to forms of xenophobia as a way of maintaining the current neo-colonial order of property relations, both at the level of the nation state and internationally. This would rely on, as it does now, uneven geography of governance: more brutal at its edges than in its heartlands. However, the tactics it might use to secure its own hegemony, in the context of the declining coherence and waning strength of that hegemony's economic fundamentals, might entail escalating towards greater violence. Although they are, for now, largely deployed in the

Global South, these tactics for maintaining order would likely eventually return to the capitalist heartlands. Much of this description could be assembled from a bricolage of theories of fascism: Samir Amin's response to crisis;[60] Mann's use of paramilitary violence;[61] and, most clearly, Aimé Césaire's theory of 'endocolonialism'.[62]

Endocolonialism is the idea that fascism is constituted by the use of the technologies of colonialism back in the colonizing states themselves – the most obvious example being the concentration camp. Such geographical inconsistencies of governance are built into 'Batteries, Bombs and Borders'. As a form of global rule, it is likely to contain localized forms of 'Fossilized Reaction', similar to how empires have been governed by inconsistent regimes of violence for centuries.

Endocolonialism, however, cannot be what it was: contemporary colonial geographies are now much more complex. Whereas until the early twentieth century European countries waged colonial wars against non-capitalist societies in what is now called the Global South, the production of a global market – an inexorable tendency of capitalist growth itself – integrated the entire globe into a single system. The fascism in 'Batteries, Bombs and Borders' can therefore only be related to the fascism of 'interwar fascism' through a process of abstraction: abstracting from the specifics of colonial rule to neo-colonial forms of governance, and then understanding the modes by which those neo-colonial governments might return to the capitalist 'core', now relativized within capitalism itself.

Future telling only gets us so far. If neither of these two futures constitutes a return to fascism directly, this is still not a comforting conclusion. Fascism, in Michael Mann's conception, is a movement that radicalizes politics further beyond conservative authoritarianism. As such, it depends on the (relatively slow) accumulation of authoritarian instruments by the conservative states that preceded it. It is far from likely that we can see from our present vantage point the forms that might eventually turn into 'ecofascism', although we can point, as we have here, to aspects of wider politics that might set the stage for its arrival.

One needs all these three aspects: the state aspect, the movement aspect, and the crisis aspect to be able to understand fascism. Such a multifaceted concept of fascism might make its opposition confusing. But, on the contrary, it can also mean that the struggle against fascism emerging in the future is also the struggle against milder forms of authoritarianism emerging now. It is to this, as well as to environmental movements – in their more hopeful variants – to which we now turn.

Conclusion

Climate change is not a single apocalyptic and remote event. It consists of a multitude of distinct transformations in nature and in humanity's relations with nature. Some of these transformations will be chronic, some acute. They will affect different people in different areas in different ways. So far, and probably for a while to come, many of those bearing the brunt – dying, or losing everything they've ever had, or having their livelihoods thrown into disarray – are in the Global South. Those who have contributed almost nothing to global climate change will suffer the most. From this profound inequity comes the essential call for climate justice.

We must, however, recognize that understanding climate change as a profoundly unequal situation has another valence. There are those who can read the words above, and all other talk of the sheer *injustice* of it all, and draw the exact opposite conclusion. Those on the far right, whose imagined interests lie exclusively with a racial group or national body, will see these massively differentiated impacts as reason to stay unconcerned, perhaps blaming those most immediately affected by it for their poverty. If they do see climate change as a threat, they will likely respond by protecting their own interests over all others. In short, assertions of the differential impacts of climate change can be read as inadvertent arguments for what Christian Parenti has called the 'politics of the armed lifeboat'.[1]

But crucially, those in the Global South will not be the only ones affected. This 'head in the sand' response is profoundly self-destructive for the far right in the Global North. The temporality of the climate crisis – past emissions continue to affect the climate for decades and centuries to come – means that the failure to mitigate now increases the severity of the inevitable destruction. Indeed, for many in the North, profound shocks are already inescapable, whether from heat waves, storms, water shortages, crop failures, supply chain disruption, forest fires, the steady migration northwards of insect disease vectors or pandemics. Insulation from the rest of the world in the context of our current logistical-extractive regime is simply not an option. Nor is it possible to isolate oneself from migration. Immediate action on climate change mitigation is the just and right position to take: it responds to the slow violence of environmental degradation which will spread to the Global North. Such action is in all our interests.

Climate systems breakdown doesn't always appear as a distinct kind of problem in its own right. One of the central challenges in the next few years might be differentiating it from other, ongoing, crises. Was Hurricane Maria due to climate change? Was the COVID-19 pandemic a product of climate systems breakdown? Was the Syrian Civil War?[2] Some might baulk at this 'Scooby-Doo environmentalism' – take the mask off a given crisis and it was climate change all along[3] – in part because it seems to render human action insignificant. But we can also draw the opposite conclusion. The purpose of understanding the climate in and through what appear to be political, military or social crises, is to understand climate change not as a natural event, merely happening *to* us, but to understand that environmental politics is saturated with decisions, both causative of climate change and responsive to it.

Climate systems breakdown will affect all the existing forms of social and political life. Because of this, many existing forms of political struggle remain relevant in the face of its consequences. The struggle for good housing still makes sense in the aftermath of floods and rising sea levels; it simply needs scaling up. The struggle for adequate care in society is still relevant in a radically decarbonized world. Indeed, the expansion of low-carbon care work might even be part of getting us there.[4] The right to nutritious food is still worth fighting for, even as harvests become more volatile. The struggle for the right to move is still relevant, and likely even more so. We must establish that 'insurance, housing, food, energy, health and social care, education, and emergency services are universal basic rights.'[5] By the same token, however, the exclusionary politics of the far right will also remain relevant. In the twenty-first century, all politics will, in one way or another, be climate politics.

Nevertheless, climate systems breakdown is not some mere recolouring of existing social problems. To borrow for a moment the language of securitization, it is a 'severe risk multiplier'. How severe? Back in 2007, before a decade and a half of upwards revisions, the normally sober Center for Strategic and International Studies and Center for a New American Security described it thus: 'unchecked climate change equals the world depicted by Mad Max, only hotter, with no beaches, and perhaps with even more chaos'.[6]

That sounds bad. Indeed, it sounds appalling. Because of the sheer scale and complexity of the climate crisis problem, it can be easy to adopt an attitude of fatalism. Future climate destruction seems 'baked in'. Against this fatalism, this book joins a chorus of those affirming that it is never too late to act, either on emissions or on their human and political consequences. Neither mitigation nor adaptation is ever 'too late'.

And even if fatalism overtakes the wider climate movement, the political settlement we live through is still up
for contestation. We must acknowledge – as many in the
climate movement have argued for years – that much of
the struggle needs to be over the conditions of adaptation.
Indeed, politics is a rather more responsive system than the
climate: major reversals of fortune can happen in spans of
a few months.

Whatever happens with the climate, it will always be
made worse by the arrival of far-right authoritarianism.
The politics of exclusion, racism, parochialism, hierarchy
and conspiracy were fundamentally inadequate to the
challenges that society faced at every point in its entire
history. There is no reason to suspect they might suddenly
be useful in the future.

None of this is to suggest that engaging with adaptation
to climate change is the only *really* important challenge, or
more important than the work of reducing emissions. We
must fight to directly reverse the emission of gigatons of
carbon into the atmosphere as well as for favourable social
adaptation. After all, in the long term, any favourable
social settlement will be undermined by a great enough
failure of mitigation: in the unimaginable stress of a 4°C
warmer world, all bets on social stability are off.

In our previous book, we concluded with reflections
on the anti-fascist movement. There, we analysed new
far-right movements that have emerged on the internet;
our discussion of anti-fascism was therefore focused on
opposing those movements, both online and off. Here we
need a rather broader scope. Some parts of our analysis,
however, remain unchanged. First, even in the context of
climate change, exploiting tensions in the far right remains
a useful strategy. Contradictions within far-right nature
politics abound, between the rural and the urban, statecraft
and mass shootings, nihilism and spirituality, the needs of
capital and the projected needs of the *Volk*.

The second is that contested cultural spaces remain
central to anti-fascism, anti-racism and the environmental

movement foremost among them. However, far from call-
ing for the simple diffusion of anti-fascist norms into these
political spaces, organized anti-fascists also have a huge
amount to learn from these struggles. The engagement
must be bidirectional. This cannot be an argument for
homogeneity in the climate movement. We can't afford it.
The anti-nuclear movement, the civil rights movement, the
feminist movement: all were or are huge and heterogeneous. Tactical/strategic heterogeneity is a source of strength
for social movements. Indeed, as we noted before, in the
case of the Civil Rights movement, the existence of multiple flanks, along with the courage and skill of its members,
arguably gave the movement its dynamism.[7]

If anti-fascism wants to be resolutely anti-fascist then it
must address climate change. If environmentalism wants
to equitably resolve the crises of climate change it must be
anti-fascist.

Any climate politics will mobilize an idea of nature.
Throughout this book, we have noted ways in which images
of nature have been mobilized by far-right actors: the idea
of a pristine, inexhaustible nature that underpinned the
expansion of colonial exploitation, the proposition of a
mystical relationship between an ethnic group and a landscape, the application of methods of animal breeding to
human reproduction, and both the absolutization of the
rights of humans and their total denigration. We must
resist those ideas of nature that are hierarchical, parochial,
tied to a certain race or divided into essentially killable and
unkillable parts.

However, at the same time, we almost certainly cannot
(neither cognitively nor politically) progress from where
we are without *some* conception of nature. Where might
we find a better understanding of nature? The sources are
many and varied: indigenous knowledge, the conceptual
resources developed under the frameworks of social ecology and ecosocialism and, perhaps most importantly of all,
biology and climate science, as well as a critical understanding of their histories. These disciplines and non-disciplines

contain an enormous repository for thinking about a nature whose political valences are not so clearly tied up with political domination. Indeed, they articulate nothing less than the basis for a common humanity. However, it is not a commonality shorn of its intertwinement with more-than-human nature. We are dependent on a particular climatic system, a fact which, for most of us, modernity has obscured, but which will become more and more clear as climate change accelerates. Thus, solidarity must extend not just to those humans and societies upon which we depend, but to the more-than-human nature that we exist within as well.

However, this is not quite enough on its own. A nature-rooted image of a common humanity without political articulation – without a clear understanding of the history of ecological domination, and without the development of new forms of connection against it – can become both reactionary (as it comes to see humans as undifferentiated, all equally to blame) or individualistic (as it attempts to 'save nature' without changing the economic structures which have driven the earth to the brink). To get us out of the traps of both reaction and individualism, we need a new, more robust, form of solidarity.

Whatever forms of parochialism are brought against it, the climate crisis remains determinedly planetary in scope. Solidarity within, at and across borders is therefore essential. Solidarity has often been articulated on the basis of equivalence – not sameness, but the quality of two people having a similar relationship to something else. In the case of the worker's movement, two workers' relationships to their workplaces – no matter what their other differences – were functionally identical and on that basis they could organize. The homogenizing effect of the worker's labour power sold on the market made it so.[8]

But it is a struggle to articulate solidarity in climate change like this. The opacities of contemporary capitalism – its vast scale and scope and the tensions between the positions we each have within it – make it difficult to articulate how we relate across this complexity. We might even say that contemporary governance relies on the heterogeneity of the ways we are attached to capitalism to keep us apart. And yet in the context of this heterogeneity, we must find solidarity.

There is also a more fundamental problem with articulating solidarity in climate change. For those in the Global North, whose share of the carbon suspended in the atmosphere is much higher than that of those living on the rest of the planet, and whose lives depend on the ongoing extraction of resources from the Global South, the politics of shame and blame are rarely popular. What is the relationship of the American or Swedish or Japanese consumer to the person sweltering in a heatwave in a Mumbai slum, or a Chilean miner extracting lithium from the ground, or a rural Chinese worker sewing garments for export? In the terms that the racist far right would have us adopt, the answer is obvious: nothing. Equally, in the language of liberalism, thought of either *as citizens* or *as consumers*, their relationship, as mediated through climate change, is also clear: they are antagonists. The carbon emissions of the society of the former are (statistically speaking) responsible for the heatwave that makes the slum so deadly. And the alleviation of the latter's suffering can seemingly only be through voluntary privation on the part of the former. The struggle the two have in common is the struggle against each other.

But this is not all that either of them is. Focusing on these moments of apparent antagonism obscures the other forms of solidarity and complex interdependence that might exist between these people – and the ecosystems they both depend on. It is precisely *against* the process of dividing humans into distinct groups of people that solidarity operates. My demand that I be able to access cheap food was always in contradiction with the demands of other people that they be paid fairly for their work in producing it. Solidarity, which was never just solidarity between workers *as workers*, was the assertion of a commonality *across* this governing division. We must refuse the idea that our common humanity depends exclusively on the roles that our existing political and economic systems would have us play.

Solidarity is an attempt to overcome the split from which governance derives its power. Governance masks prior unity, a unity we argued above could be found in new ideas of nature. In this way, solidarity and a particular image of nature depend on each other, but neither is entirely sufficient alone. A particular idea of nature cannot produce solidarity, but solidarity cannot pose a unity to be constructed or recovered without a particular understanding of our unity in nature.[9] As Jason Moore writes, 'The history of justice in the twenty-first century will turn on how well we can identify these antagonisms and mutual interdependencies, and how adeptly we can build political coalitions that transcend these planetary contradictions.'[10]

Solidarity is not *just* an obligation. It should also be a mode of enlivening, a mode of extracting ourselves from our parochialism and opening out into the planetary ecology we collectively live through. It must be – as the poet Keston Sutherland wrote of love – 'made from scratch at the first sign of its possibility'.[11] The reconceptualization of solidarity to allow for its articulation of commonality across huge time-scales, which were so important to make the case for colonial reparations, must also be used for finding solidarity amidst the vast, seemingly intractable network of complex causes and effects which defines the climate crisis. Of course, the effects of climate change and colonialism are deeply intertwined. We need further and fuller articulations of this kind of solidarity-in-difference: alive to the multiplicity of ways through which we interact and interdepend across vast networks of the more-than-human.

Nevertheless, within this complexity, our subjection to capitalism is not equal. We should not be seduced into thinking that 'climate change is either a "national" problem or one of "humanity" as an undifferentiated mass'.[12]

It is not, perhaps, a relationship between 'humans' and nature that we should understand as the cause of our predicament, but the relationship between human *activity* and nature. And it is not human activity *as a whole* that we need to contend with but *humans fulfilling capitalism's imperative to endless expansion of production and extraction through the cheapening of nature*: extracting oil and rare earth minerals, radically simplifying ecologies to afford extraction, burning the Amazon for cattle farming and so on.

As Jason Moore writes, planetary justice depends on establishing justice between two points. On the one hand, there is the 'crisis of cheap nature', in which 'nature stops being cheap and starts mounting ever-more effective resistance'. And, at the same time, there's also resistance to 'cheapening in the sense of cultural domination', built on the class, race and gendered inequalities which are used to govern. 'Among the most central problems of planetary justice today is to forge a strategy that links justice across and through these two moments.'[13]

Equally, it is imperative for us to fight against frameworks that place particular races of people as the cause of inequality, disenfranchisement or ecological collapse. Antisemitism, the 'ecosocialism of fools', has been characterized as a 'refusal to see the targeted issues as fully systemic and instead focuses on specific actors, often Jews or roles and labels commonly associated with Jews, and thereby import traditional antisemitic bigotries in the name of a liberatory politics'.[14] To fight against not only these forms of hatred, but against the possibility of them taking on vaster power, we must contend with capitalism and with private property as the central institution which has enabled capitalism to bring us to our current disaster.

Time is, nevertheless, against us. *Ad hoc*, voluntarist approaches to solidarity not only fail to meet the scale of the climate crisis, they collapse when they run out of steam, which simply isn't viable on the time-frame demanded, namely *for the rest of our lives*. We must therefore engage with and attempt to repurpose existing institutions. Christian Parenti argues that a resolution to the climate crisis must be built through the institutions that currently exist, because no others are possible to construct in sufficient time: 'Either capitalism solves the crisis, or it destroys civilization. ... We cannot wait for a socialist, or communist, or anarchist, or deep-ecology, neoprimitive revolution.'[15]

But justice must nevertheless be sought in and through both the mitigation of, and adaptation to, climate systems breakdown. The left cannot give up on its other aims because the climate crisis overrules them. Justice, redistribution, the expansion of civil rights, and the empowerment of those most vulnerable to climate breakdown should be at the heart of the ecological movement. Indeed, as the struggles of Indigenous peoples against the construction of oil pipelines across their lands in North America have shown, much of the time, they already are.

Even as we recognize that this language is anathema to the far right, we must persist with it. Indeed, the language of justice, as well as the critique of private property rights, might, as Samir Gandesha advises, allow us to separate ourselves from the right's critique of capitalism as a nebulous force opposing itself to the national community.[16] We must be clear about capitalism and the rejection of private property – because the far right cannot be.

Murray Bookchin, in a lecture given in 1978 warning against the influence of Garrett Hardin's 1974 essay 'Lifeboat Ethics: the Case Against Helping the Poor', outlines his way of engaging with the world: 'What I am concerned with is, again, what is liberatory, what is ecological.'[17] As are we. And yet, as we discussed in our first chapter on the history of 'right-environmentalism', the right has also had its uses for 'ecologies'. We identified 'far-right ecologism' with a particular formula: the production and maintenance of racial hierarchy in and through nature. Stating our antagonist like this, our path perhaps becomes clearer. We must identify, defend and amplify ecological relations which restore and respect natural systems whilst attacking systems of private ownership of the means of production and attempting to re-common the world. It is incumbent upon all of us to prepare ourselves for the coming crisis, and all the attendant politics it will bring.

Perhaps anti-fascism in the climate crisis consists of this: that we oppose ecologies of domination with ecologies of liberation. The scope of such an ecology must not be contained to a particular locale, but be planetary, or even larger. 'Far-right ecologists', 'ecofascists': both would say that what matters in a given ecology is particular racial blood ties, under whose spell all forms of domination and solidarity must work. Although their politics can seem mythic in stature, grandiose even, faced with the complexity and depth of the real natural world, and the real lives humans and all other life can live through it, it is the politics of the far right that is – in truth – the most deeply parochial.

Notes

Introduction

1 Robert M. Beyer, Andrea Manica and Camilo Mora, 'Shifts in Global Bat Diversity Suggest a Possible Role of Climate Change in the Emergence of SARS-CoV-1 and SARS-CoV-2'. *Science of The Total Environment*, 26 January 2021, 145413. See also Rob Wallace, *Dead Epidemiologists: On the Origins of Covid-19* (New York: Monthly Review Press, 2020).
2 Umberto Eco, 'Ur-Fascism'. *New York Review of Books*, 22 June 1995.
3 Andreas Malm, *How to Blow up a Pipeline: Learning to Fight in a World on Fire* (Brooklyn, NY: Verso, 2020), p. 54.
4 See Sam Moore and Alex Roberts, *Post-Internet Far Right* (London: Dog Section Press, 2021), Introduction.
5 Clive Hamilton, *Requiem for a Species* (Crows Nest, NSW: Allen & Unwin, 2010), p. 209.
6 Geoff Mann and Joel Wainwright, *Climate Leviathan: A Political Theory of Our Planetary Future* (New York: Verso, 2018).
7 Andreas Malm and the Zetkin Collective, *White Skin, Black Fuel: On the Danger of Fossil Fascism* (New York: Verso, 2021).

8 For example, Mathew Lawrence and Laurie Laybourn-Langton, *Planet on Fire: A Manifesto for the Age of Environmental Breakdown* (New York: Verso, 2021).

9 Bernhard Forchtner, 'Eco-Fascism "Proper": The Curious Case of Greenline Front', Centre for Analysis of the Radical Right, 25 June 2020, https://www.radicalrightanalysis.com/2020/06/25/eco-fascism-proper-the-curious-case-of-greenline-front/.

10 James Delingpole, *The Little Green Book of Eco-Fascism: The Left's Plan to Frighten Your Kids, Drive Up Energy Costs and Hike Your Taxes!* (London: Biteback Publishing, 2014).

11 Frank Uekötter, *The Green and the Brown: A History of Conservation in Nazi Germany*, Illustrated edition (Cambridge: Cambridge University Press, 2006), p. 14.

12 For example, Murray Bookchin, 'Social Ecology versus Deep Ecology: A Challenge for the Ecology Movement'. *Green Perspectives: Newsletter of the Green Program Project*, Summer 1987.

13 Keith Mako Woodhouse, *The Ecocentrists: A History of Radical Environmentalism* (New York: Columbia University Press, 2018), p. 2.

14 Ibid, p. 196.

15 Ibid.

16 Ben Makuch, 'Fascists Impersonate Climate Group to Say Coronavirus Is Good for Earth'. *VICE News*, 25 March 2020. https://www.vice.com/en/article/n7jmmx/fascists-impersonate-climate-group-to-say-coronavirus-is-good-for-earth.

17 Emily Atkin, 'The Antler Guy Isn't a Climate Activist. He's an Eco-Fascist'. *HEATED* (blog), 11 January 2021. https://heated.world/p/the-antler-guy-isnt-a-climate-activist; Jules Evans, 'A Closer Look at the "QAnon Shaman" Leading the Mob'. *GEN* (blog), 7 January 2021. https://gen.medium.com/the-q-shaman-conspirituality-goes-rioting-on-capitol-hill-24bac5fc50e6.

18 Charlotte Ward and Prof David Voas, 'The Emergence of Conspirituality'. *Journal of Contemporary Religion* 26, no. 1 (2011): 103–21; see also Egil Asprem and Asbjørn Dyrendal, 'Conspirituality Reconsidered: How Surprising and How New Is the Confluence of Spirituality and Conspiracy Theory?'. *Journal of Contemporary Religion* 30, no. 3 (2015): 367–82.

19 Bernhard Forchtner, 'Eco-Fascism: Justifications of Terrorist Violence in the Christchurch Mosque Shooting and the El Paso Shooting'. *OpenDemocracy*, 13 August 2019. https://www.opendemocracy.net/en/countering-radi cal-right/eco-fascism-justifications-terrorist-violence-christ church-mosque-shooting-and-el-paso-shooting/.

20 Michael Mann, *Fascists* (Cambridge: Cambridge University Press, 2004), p. 13.

21 David Renton, *Fascism: History and Theory* (London: Pluto Press, 2020); see also Dylan Riley, *The Civic Foundations of Fascism in Europe*, reprint edn (Baltimore, MD: Verso Books, 2019).

22 George L. Mosse, *The Crisis of German Ideology: Intellectual Origins of the Third Reich* (New York: Schocken Books, 1981).

23 Samir Amin, 'The Return of Fascism in Contemporary Capitalism', *Monthly Review*, 1 September 2014; see also Aimé Césaire, *Discourse on Colonialism* (New York: Monthly Review Press, 2000).

24 Robert O. Paxton, *The Anatomy of Fascism* (New York: Alfred A. Knopf, 2004), p. 42.

25 Jonathan Olsen, *Nature and Nationalism* (New York: Palgrave Macmillan, 1999).

26 Balša Lubarda, 'Beyond Ecofascism? Far-Right Ecologism (FRE) as a Framework for Future Inquiries'. *Environmental Values* 29, no. 6 (2020): 713–32.

27 Ibid.

Chapter 1: A history of far-right ecologism

1 W.E.B. Du Bois, 'The Souls of White Folk'. In *Writings*, ed. by Nathan Irvin Huggins (New York: The Library of America, 1986), 923–38.

2 For a theoretical exposition, see Sverker Sörlin and Nina Wormbs, 'Environing Technologies: A Theory of Making Environment'. *History and Technology* 34, no. 2 (2018): 101–25.

3 Lucas Stephens, Dorian Fuller, Nicole Boivin, et al. 'Archaeological Assessment Reveals Earth's Early Transformation through Land Use'. *Science* 365, no. 6456 (2019): 897–902.

4 Michael McCormick, Ulf Büntgen, Mark A. Cane, et al. 'Climate Change during and after the Roman Empire: Reconstructing the Past from Scientific and Historical Evidence'. *Journal of Interdisciplinary History* xliii, no. 2 (2012): 169–220.

5 Raj Patel and Jason W. Moore, *A History of the World in Seven Cheap Things: A Guide to Capitalism, Nature, and the Future of the Planet* (Berkeley, CA: University of California Press, 2020). For a more theoretically dense account, see Jason W. Moore, *Capitalism in the Web of Life: Ecology and the Accumulation of Capital* (New York: Verso, 2015).

6 Jason W. Moore (ed.), *Anthropocene or Capitalocene? Nature, History, and the Crisis of Capitalism* (Oakland, CA: PM Press, 2016).

7 This history of nature in colonialism is contrasting but complementary to that offered in Malm and the Zetkin Collective, *White Skin*, especially the chapter 'Skin and Fuel'. Where we emphasize the production of power through ecologies and ideas of nature, they focus on the domination afforded by nature's exploitation.

8 Ellen Meiksins Wood, *The Origin of Capitalism: A Longer View* (London: Verso, 2002).

9 Roger J. P. Kain, John Chapman, and Richard R. Oliver, *The Enclosure Maps of England and Wales, 1595–1918* (Cambridge: Cambridge University Press, 2004), pp. 4–5.

10 Brett M. Bennett and Gregory A. Barton, 'The Enduring Link between Forest Cover and Rainfall: A Historical Perspective on Science and Policy Discussions'. *Forest Ecosystems* 5, no. 1 (2018), p. 5.

11 Richard Grove, *Ecology, Climate, and Empire: Colonialism and Global Environmental History, 1400–1940* (Cambridge: White Horse Press, 1997), p. 39.

12 Richard Grove, *Green Imperialism: Colonial Expansion, Tropical Island Edens, and the Origins of Environmentalism, 1600–1860* (Cambridge: Cambridge University Press, 1995), p. 276.

13 Grove, *Ecology, Climate*, p. 48.

14 Richard Drayton, *Nature's Government: Science, Imperial Britain, and the 'Improvement' of the World* (New Haven, CT: Yale University Press, 2000).

15 Grove, *Ecology, Climate*, p. 39.
16 Grove, *Green Imperialism*, p. 278.
17 Ibid., p. 276.
18 Nicholas Beuret, 'Containing Climate Change: The New Governmental Strategies of Catastrophic Environments'. *Environment and Planning E: Nature and Space*, January 2020, doi: 10.1177/2514848620902384, p. 4.
19 Ibid., p. 5.
20 Thomas Malthus, *An Essay on the Principle of Population* (London: Electronic Scholarly Publishing Project, 1998).
21 Kevin Hjortshøj O'Rourke, 'Migration and the Escape from Malthus'. *Critical Quarterly* 57, no. 3 (2015): 93–7.
22 Grove, *Ecology, Climate*, p. 42.
23 John McNeill, *Mosquito Empires: Ecology and War in the Greater Caribbean, 1620–1914* (Cambridge: Cambridge University Press, 2010).
24 Daniel Clayton and Gavin Bowd, 'Geography, Tropicality and Postcolonialism: Anglophone and Francophone Readings of the Work of Pierre Gourou'. *L'Espace geographique* 35, no. 3 (2006): 208–21.
25 Bain Attwood, 'Law, History and Power: The British Treatment of Aboriginal Rights in Land in New South Wales'. *The Journal of Imperial and Commonwealth History* 42, no. 1 (2014): 171–92.
26 Grove, *Green Imperialism*, pp. 282–8.
27 David N. Livingstone, 'Race, Space and Moral Climatology: Notes toward a Genealogy'. *Journal of Historical Geography* 28, no. 2 (2002): 159–80, p. 161.
28 James Fairhead, Melissa Leach and Ian Scoones, 'Green Grabbing: A New Appropriation of Nature?' *Journal of Peasant Studies* 39, no. 2 (2012): 237–61.
29 Ramachandra Guha, *The Unquiet Woods: Ecological Change and Peasant Resistance in the Himalaya* (Ranikhet: Permanent Black, 2010).
30 Caroline C. Ford, *Natural Interests: The Contest over the Environment in Modern France* (Cambridge, MA: Harvard University Press, 2016).
31 Isaac Kantor, 'Ethnic Cleansing and America's Creation of National Parks'. *Public Land & Resources Law Review* 28 (2007): 42–64.
32 Grove, *Ecology, Climate*, p. 43.

33 Ibid., p. 183.
34 Alfred W. Crosby, *Ecological Imperialism: The Biological Expansion of Europe, 900–1900* (Cambridge: Cambridge University Press, 2004).
35 Simon Lewis and Mark Maslin, 'Defining the Anthropocene'. *Nature* 519 (2015): 171–80.
36 Jairus Victor Grove, *Savage Ecology: War and Geopolitics at the End of the World* (Durham, NC: Duke University Press, 2019), ch. 3; David D. Smits, 'The Frontier Army and the Destruction of the Buffalo: 1865–1883'. *The Western Historical Quarterly* 25, no. 3 (1994): 312–38.
37 Roxanne Dunbar-Ortiz, *An Indigenous Peoples' History of the United States* (Boston, MA: Beacon Press, 2014), p. 144.
38 Stephen J. Gould, *The Mismeasure of Man*, rev. and exp. edn (New York: W.W. Norton & Company, 1996), p. 379.
39 Jonathan Peter Spiro, *Defending the Master Race: Conservation, Eugenics, and the Legacy of Madison Grant* (Burlington, VT: University of Vermont Press, 2009), p. 106.
40 Martin Woodroffe, 'Racial Theories of History and Politics: The Example of Houston Stewart Chamberlain'. In Paul M. Kennedy and Anthony James Nicholls (eds.), *Nationalist and Racialist Movements in Britain and Germany Before 1914* (Basingstoke: Palgrave Macmillan, 1981), 143–53, pp. 145–6.
41 Spiro, *Defending the Master Race*, p. 115.
42 John Nale, 'Arthur de Gobineau on Blood and Race'. *Critical Philosophy of Race* 2, no. 1 (2014): 106–24, p. 111; Yasuko Takezawa, Audrey Smedley and Peter Wade, 'Race'. In *Encyclopedia Britannica*.
43 Spiro, *Defending the Master Race*, p. 124.
44 Thomas Moynihan, *X-Risk: How Humanity Discovered Its Own Extinction* (Falmouth: Urbanomic, 2020).
45 Russell McGregor, 'The Doomed Race: A Scientific Axiom of the Late Nineteenth Century'. *Australian Journal of Politics & History* 39, no. 1 (1993): 14–22.
46 Daniel J. Kevles, *In the Name of Eugenics: Genetics and the Uses of Human Heredity* (Cambridge, MA: Harvard University Press, 1995), p. 4.
47 Mike Hawkins, *Social Darwinism in European and*

American Thought, 1860–1945: Nature as Model and Nature as Threat (Cambridge: Cambridge University Press, 1997), pp. 217–18.

48 Alexandra Minna Stern, *Eugenic Nation: Faults and Frontiers of Better Breeding in Modern America* (Oakland, CA: University of California Press, 2016), p. 3.

49 James Q. Whitman, *Hitler's American Model: The United States and the Making of Nazi Race Law*, illus. edn (Princeton, NJ: Princeton University Press, 2017).

50 Spiro, *Defending the Master Race*, p. 8.

51 Ibid., p. 53.

52 Ibid., p. 6.

53 Ibid., p. 157.

54 Ibid., p. 115.

55 Mosse, *Crisis of German Ideology*, p. 15.

56 Adam Knowles, *Heidegger's Fascist Affinities: A Politics of Silence* (Stanford, CA: Stanford University Press, 2019), pp. 36–8.

57 Mark Bassin, 'Blood or Soil?' In Franz-Josef Brüggemeier, Mark Cioc and Thomas Zeller (eds.), *How Green Were the Nazis? Nature, Environment, and Nation in the Third Reich* (Athens, OH: Ohio University Press, 2005), 204–42, p. 207.

58 Peter Staudenmaier, 'Fascist Ecology: The "Green Wing" of the Nazi Party and Its Historical Antecedents'. In *Ecofascism: Lessons from the German Experience* (Chico, CA: AK Press, 1996).

59 Mosse, *Crisis of German Ideology*, p. 19.

60 Charles E. Closmann, 'Legalizing a Volksgemeinschaft: Nazi Germany's Reich Nature Protection Law of 1935'. In Franz-Josef Brüggemeier, Mark Cioc and Thomas Zeller (eds.), *How Green Were the Nazis? Nature, Environment, and Nation in the Third Reich* (Athens, OH: Ohio University Press, 2005), p. 24.

61 Richard J. Evans, *The Coming of the Third Reich* (New York: The Penguin Press, 2009).

62 Mosse, *Crisis of German Ideology*, p. 7.

63 Dan Stone, *The Holocaust, Fascism and Memory: Essays in the History of Ideas* (Basingstoke: Palgrave Macmillan, 2013), p. 110.

64 Paxton, *Anatomy of Fascism*, p. 71.

65 For an extended discussion of the role of cheap food, see Moore, *Capitalism in the Web of Life*.

66 Paxton, *Anatomy of Fascism*, pp. 71–4. See also Robert O. Paxton, *French Peasant Fascism: Henry Dorgère's Greenshirts and the Crises of French Agriculture, 1929–1939* (New York: Oxford University Press, 1997).

67 Philip M. Coupland, *Farming, Fascism and Ecology: A Life of Jorian Jenks* (London: Routledge, 2017), p. 289.

68 Ibid., pp. 82, 97.

69 Ibid., p. 287.

70 Stone, *Holocaust, Fascism and Memory*, p. 106.

71 Peter Hay, *Main Currents in Western Environmental Thought* (Bloomington, IN: Indiana University Press, 2002), p. 184.

72 Wilko Graf von Hardenberg, 'A Nation's Parks: Failure and Success in Fascist Nature Conservation'. *Modern Italy* 19, no. 3 (2014): 275–85, p. 275.

73 Marco Armiero, 'Introduction: Fascism and Nature'. *Modern Italy* 19, no. 3 (2014): 241–5.

74 Federico Caprotti and Maria Kaïka, 'Producing the Ideal Fascist Landscape: Nature, Materiality and the Cinematic Representation of Land Reclamation in the Pontine Marshes'. *Social & Cultural Geography* 9, no. 6 (2008): 613–34.

75 Federico Caprotti, 'The Invisible War on Nature: The Abyssinian War (1935–1936) in Newsreels and Documentaries in Fascist Italy'. *Modern Italy* 19, no. 3 (2014): 305–21, p. 307.

76 Caprotti and Kaïka, 'Producing the Ideal Fascist Landscape'.

77 Ian Kershaw, '"Working Towards the Führer". Reflections on the Nature of the Hitler Dictatorship'. *Contemporary European History* 2, no. 2 (1993): 103–18, p. 109.

78 Charles E. Closmann, 'Environment', in Shelley Baranowski, Armin Nolzen and Claus-Christian W. Szejnmann (eds.), *A Companion to Nazi Germany* (New York: Wiley-Blackwell, 2018), 413–28, p. 417.

79 Richard J. Evans, *The Third Reich in Power, 1933–1939* (New York: Penguin Press, 2005), pp. 338–9.

80 Peter Staudenmaier, 'Advocates for the Landscape: Alwin Seifert and Nazi Environmentalism'. *German Studies Review* 43, no. 2 (2020): 271–90.

81 Charles E. Closmann, 'Legalizing a Volksgemeinschaft: Nazi Germany's Reich Nature Protection Law of 1935'. In Franz-Josef Brüggemcier, Mark Cioc and Thomas Zeller (eds.). *How Green Were the Nazis? Nature, Environment, and Nation in the Third Reich* (Athens, OH: Ohio University Press, 2005), p. 20.

82 Joachim Radkau, *Nature and Power: A Global History of the Environment* (Cambridge: Cambridge University Press, 2008), p. 265.

83 Franz-Josef Brüggemeier, Mark Cioc and Thomas Zeller, 'Introduction', in Franz-Josef Brüggemeier, Mark Cioc and Thomas Zeller (eds.), *How Green Were the Nazis? Nature, Environment, and Nation in the Third Reich* (Athens, OH: Ohio University Press, 2005), 1–17, p. 10.

84 Closmann, 'Environment', p. 418.

85 Staudenmaier, 'Advocates for the Landscape'.

86 Ibid., p. 274.

87 Peter Staudenmaier, 'Organic Farming in Nazi Germany: The Politics of Biodynamic Agriculture, 1933–1945'. *Environmental History* 18, no. 2 (2013): 383–411.

88 Michael E. Zimmerman, 'The Threat of Ecofascism'. *Social Theory and Practice* 21, no. 2 (1995): 207–38.

89 Michael E. Zimmerman, J. Baird Callicott, John Clark, Karen J. Warren and Irene J. Klaver, *Environmental Philosophy: From Animal Rights to Radical Ecology* (Upper Saddle River, NJ: Pearson, 2004), p. 395.

90 Mann, *Fascists*, p. 15.

91 Timothy Snyder, *Black Earth: The Holocaust as History and Warning* (London: Vintage, 2016), ch. 1.

92 Ibid., p. 26.

93 Mann, *The Sources of Social Power: Volume 3 Global Empires and Revolution, 1890–1945* (Cambridge: Cambridge University Press, 1993), p. 217; Evans, *Coming of the Third Reich*, 'The Hyperinflation'.

94 Evans, *Coming of the Third Reich*, 'Rebuilding the movement'.

95 Ibid.

96 Most famously, Anna Bramwell, *Blood and Soil: Richard Walther Darré and Hitler's 'Green Party'* (Abbotsbrook: Kensal Press, 1985).

97 Gesine Gerhard, 'Breeding Pigs and People for the Third

Reich'. In Franz-Josef Brüggemeier, Mark Cioc and Thomas Zeller (eds.), *How Green Were the Nazis? Nature, Environment, and Nation in the Third Reich* (Athens, OH: Ohio University Press, 2005), 129–46, p. 130. See also Piers H. G. Stephens, 'Blood, Not Soil: Anna Bramwell and the Myth of "Hitler's Green Party"'. *Organization & Environment* 14, no. 2 (2001): 173–87.

98 Joachim Wolschke-Bulmahn, 'Violence as the Basis of National Socialist Landscape Planning in the "Annexed Eastern Areas"'. In Franz-Josef Brüggemeier, Mark Cioc and Thomas Zeller (eds.), *How Green Were the Nazis? Nature, Environment, and Nation in the Third Reich* (Athens, OH: Ohio University Press, 2005), 243–56, p. 245.

99 Ibid., p. 243.

100 Staudenmaier, 'Advocates for the Landscape', p. 279.

101 Paxton, *Anatomy of Fascism*, p. 147.

102 Tim Cole, '"Nature Was Helping Us": Forests, Trees, and Environmental Histories of the Holocaust'. *Environmental History* 19, no. 4 (2014): 665–86. See also Andreas Malm, 'In Wildness Is the Liberation of the World: On Maroon Ecology and Partisan Nature'. *Historical Materialism* 26, no. 3 (2018): 3–37.

103 Robin D.G. Kelley, 'A Poetics of Anticolonialism'. In Aimé Césaire, *Discourse on Colonialism* (New York: Monthly Review Press, 2000), p. 8.

104 Clayton and Bowd, 'Geography, Tropicality and Postcolonialism'.

105 Will Steffen, Regina Angelina Sanderson, Peter D. Tyson, et al. *Global Change and the Earth System: A Planet Under Pressure* (Berlin: Springer Science & Business Media, 2006), p. 131; Kathy Hibbard, Paul Crutzen, Eric Lambin, Diana Liverman, Nathan Mantua, John McNeill, Bruno Messerli and Will Steffen, 'Decadal-Scale Interactions of Humans and the Environment'. In Will Steffen, Robert Constanza and Lisa Graumlich (eds.), *Sustainability or Collapse? An Integrated History and Future of People on Earth* (Cambridge, MA: MIT Press, 2006).

106 Joachim Radkau, *The Age of Ecology: A Global History* (Cambridge: Polity, 2014).

107 Eileen McGurty, *Transforming Environmentalism: Warren*

County, PCBs, and the Origins of Environmental Justice (New Brunswick, NJ: Rutgers University Press, 2009).

108 See David N. Pellow, *What Is Critical Environmental Justice?* (Cambridge: Polity, 2018) and Rob Nixon, *Slow Violence and the Environmentalism of the Poor* (Cambridge, MA: Harvard University Press, 2013).

109 Malm and the Zetkin Collective, *White Skin, Black Fuel.*

110 Coupland, *Farming, Fascism and Ecology*, pp. 199–215.

111 Axel Zutz, 'Harmonising Environmentalism and Modernity: Landscape Advocates and Scenic Embedding in Germany, c. 1920–1950'. *National Identities* 16, no. 3 (2014): 269–81.

112 Nicholas Goodrick-Clarke, *Hitler's Priestess: Savitri Devi, the Hindu-Aryan Myth and Neo-Nazism* (New York: New York University Press, 2000), pp. 131–2.

113 Tamir Bar-On, *Where Have All the Fascists Gone?* (Burlington, VT: Ashgate, 2007), p. 3.

114 Jean-Yves Camus, 'Alain de Benoist and the New Right'. In Mark J. Sedgwick (ed.), *Key Thinkers of the Radical Right: Behind the New Threat to Liberal Democracy* (New York: Oxford University Press, 2019), 73–90, p. 75.

115 Bernhard Forchtner, 'Protecting the Natural Environment? A Look at the Radical Right'. *Europe Now*, 2 October 2018. https://www.europenowjournal.org/2018/10/01/pro tecting-the-natural-environment-a-look-at-the-radical-right/.

116 Jean-Louis Prat, 'La Décroissance Est-Elle Réactionnaire?' *Revue Du MAUSS Permanente*, 10 April 2008. http:// www.journaldumauss.net/?La-Decroissance-est-elle. See also Alain de Benoist, *Décroissance, Ou, Toujours plus? Penser l'écologie Jusqu'au Bout* (Paris: Pierre-Guillaume de Roux, 2018).

117 Stéphane François, 'Guillaume Faye and Archeofuturism'. In Mark J. Sedgwick (ed.), *Key Thinkers of the Radical Right: Behind the New Threat to Liberal Democracy* (New York: Oxford University Press, 2019), 91–101, p. 96.

118 Roger Griffin, 'Between Metapolitics and Apoliteia : The Nouvelle Droite's Strategy for Conserving the Fascist Vision in the "Interregnum"'. *Modern & Contemporary France* 8, no. 1 (2000): 35–53.

119 Ian Coates, 'Cuckoo in the Nest: The National Front and Green Ideology'. In Jane Holder, Pauline Lane, Sally

Eden, Rachel Reeve, Ute Collier and Kevin Anderson (eds.), *Perspectives on the Environment: Interdisciplinary Research in Action* (Aldershot: Avebury, 1993), 13–23.

120 Janet Biehl, '"Ecology" and the Modernization of Fascism in the German Ultra-Right'. In *Ecofascism: Lessons from the German Experience* (Chico, CA: AK Press, 1996).

121 Robyn Eckersley, 'Environmentalism and Patriotism: An Unholy Alliance?' In Igor Primoratz and Aleksandar Pavkovi (eds.), *Patriotism: Philosophical and Political Perspectives* (Burlington, VT: Ashgate, 2008).

122 Erik M. Conway and Naomi Oreskes, *Merchants of Doubt: How a Handful of Scientists Obscured the Truth on Issues from Tobacco Smoke to Global Warming* (London: Bloomsbury Paperbacks, 2012), p. 177.

123 Paul R. Ehrlich, *The Population Bomb* (New York: Ballantine Books, 1968).

124 For a thorough overview of the Green Revolution, including a critique of its claims to such a substantial expansion in productivity, see Raj Patel, 'The Long Green Revolution'. *The Journal of Peasant Studies* 40, no. 1 (2013): 1–63.

125 Betsy Hartmann, *Reproductive Rights and Wrongs: The Global Politics of Population Control* (Chicago, IL: Haymarket Books, 2016).

126 Garrett Hardin, 'The Tragedy of the Commons'. *Science* 162, no. 3859 (1968): 1243–8.

127 Elinor Ostrom, *Governing the Commons: The Evolution of Institutions for Collective Action* (Cambridge: Cambridge University Press, 1990).

128 Garrett Hardin, 'Lifeboat Ethics: The Case Against Helping the Poor'. *Psychology Today* (1974): 800–12.

129 John Hultgren, *Border Walls Gone Green: Nature and Anti-Immigrant Politics in America* (Minneapolis, MN: University of Minnesota Press, 2015), p. 70.

130 Ibid.

131 Philip Cafaro, 'Book Review of "Can Life Prevail? A Revolutionary Approach to the Environmental Crisis", by Pentti Linkola'. *Environmental Values* 21 (2012): 534–6.

132 Evangelos D. Protopapadakis, 'Environmental Ethics and Linkola's Ecofascism: An Ethics Beyond Humanism'. *Frontiers of Philosophy in China* 9, no. 4 (2014): 586–601, p. 592.

133   Edward Abbey, 'Theory of Anarchy'. In *One Life at a Time, Please* (New York: Henry Holt and Company, 1988).

134   Edward Abbey, 'Immigration and Liberal Taboos'. In *One Life at a Time, Please* (New York: Henry Holt and Company, 1988).

135   Woodhouse, *Ecocentrists*, pp. 90–1.

136   Conway and Oreskes, *Merchants of Doubt*, p. 183.

137   Ibid., p. 186

138   Michael Mann and Tom Toles, *The Madhouse Effect: How Climate Change Denial Is Threatening Our Planet, Destroying Our Politics, and Driving Us Crazy* (New York: Columbia University Press, 2018), pp. 69–72.

139   For a more detailed history, see Malm, *How to Blow up a Pipeline*; James Morton Turner and Andrew C. Isenberg, *The Republican Reversal: Conservatives and the Environment from Nixon to Trump* (Cambridge, MA: Harvard University Press, 2018); and Peter J. Jacques, Riley E. Dunlap and Mark Freeman, 'The Organisation of Denial: Conservative Think Tanks and Environmental Scepticism'. *Environmental Politics* 17, no. 3 (2008): 349–85.

140   Genesis 1:28, King James Version.

141   Joseph Masco, *The Theater of Operations: National Security Affect from the Cold War to the War on Terror* (Durham, NC: Duke University Press, 2014), p. 105.

142   Ibid., p. 79.

143   Ibid., p. 107.

144   Ben Hayes, 'Colonising the Future: Climate Change and International Security Strategies'. In Nick Buxton, Ben Hayes and Susan George (eds.), *The Secure and the Dispossessed: How the Military and Corporations Are Shaping a Climate-Changed World* (London: Pluto Press, 2016), 39–62, p. 40.

145   Betsy Hartmann, 'Strategic Scarcity: The Origin and Impact of Environmental Conflict Ideas'. London School of Economics and Political Science (2002).

146   Robert D. Kaplan, 'The Coming Anarchy'. *The Atlantic*, 1 February 1994. https://www.theatlantic.com/magazine/archive/1994/02/the-coming-anarchy/304670/.

147   James O'Connor, 'The Second Contradiction of Capitalism, with an Addendum on the Two Contradictions

of Capitalism'. In *Natural Causes: Essays in Ecological Marxism* (New York: Guilford Press, 1998), pp. 158–77.

148 Ronald J. Deibert, 'From Deep Black to Green? Demystifying the Military Monitoring of the Environment'. In *Environmental Change and Security Project Report* (Woodrow Wilson Centre, 1996), p. 29; see also Betsy Hartmann, 'Population, Environment and Security: A New Trinity'. *Environment and Urbanization* 10, no. 2 (1998): 113–28.

Chapter 2: The far right and nature now

1 Sociologist Michael Mann has argued most convincingly for the importance of paramilitarism to fascism, defining fascism as 'the pursuit of a transcendent and cleansing nation-statism through paramilitarism'. Mann, *Fascists*, p. 13.

2 In our previous book, we discussed the historical modulation of this contestation of the state. Moore and Roberts, *Post-Internet Far Right*, especially chs 6, 7 and 8.

3 Ibid., chs 2, 3 and 7.

4 See Kathleen Belew, *Bring the War Home: The White Power Movement and Paramilitary America* (Cambridge, MA: Harvard University Press, 2018) for the changes in the post-1983 White Power movement; Moore and Roberts, *Post-Internet Far Right*, chs 4, 7 and 8 for more recent changes.

5 Wendy Brown, *In the Ruins of Neoliberalism: The Rise of Antidemocratic Politics in the West* (New York: Columbia University Press, 2019).

6 On ideological 'thinness', see Cas Mudde's study of populism: Cas Mudde, 'The Populist Zeitgeist'. *Government and Opposition* 39, no. 4 (2004): 541–63. On nature as a thin ideological notion for the far right, see Lubarda, 'Beyond Ecofascism?'.

7 Bernhard Forchtner, 'Far Right Articulations of The Natural Environment', in Bernhard Forchtner (ed.), *The Far Right and the Environment* (Abingdon: Routledge, 2019), p. 1.

8 Larry Lohmann, 'Neoliberalism's Climate'. In *Handbook of Neoliberalism* (Abingdon: Routledge, 2016).

9 Ibid.

10 Cf. Malm and the Zetkin Collective, *White Skin, Black Fuel*, which focuses on the racialization and 'nationalization' of fossil fuels.

11 Brown, *In the Ruins of Neoliberalism*.

12 Robert Fletcher, 'Capitalizing on Chaos: Climate Change and Disaster Capitalism'. *Ephemera* 12, no. 1/2 (2012): 97–112; Beuret, 'Containing Climate Change'; Lohmann, 'Neoliberalism's Climate'.

13 Bernhard Forchtner, 'Climate Change and the Far Right'. *Wiley Interdisciplinary Reviews: Climate Change* 10, no. 5 (2019): e604.

14 Neil Davidson and Richard Saull, 'Neoliberalism and the Far-Right: A Contradictory Embrace'. *Critical Sociology* 43, no. 4–5 (2017): 707–24.

15 Forchtner, 'Climate Change', p. 7.

16 Davidson and Saull, 'Neoliberalism and the Far-Right'.

17 Brown, *In the Ruins of Neoliberalism*.

18 Malm and the Zetkin Collective, *White Skin, Black Fuel*, p. xiii.

19 Matthew Lockwood, 'Right-Wing Populism and the Climate Change Agenda: Exploring the Linkages'. *Environmental Politics* 27, no. 4 (2018): 712–32.

20 Malm and the Zetkin Collective, *White Skin, Black Fuel*, pp. 118–31.

21 Jeremy Schulman, 'Every Insane Thing Donald Trump Has Said about Global Warming'. Mother Jones, 12 December 2018. https://www.motherjones.com/environment/2016/12/trump-climate-timeline/.

22 Nadja Popovich, Livia Albeck-Ripka and Kendra Pierre-Louis, 'The Trump Administration Rolled Back More Than 100 Environmental Rules. Here's the Full List'. *The New York Times*, 16 October 2020, https://www.nytimes.com/interactive/2020/climate/trump-environment-rollbacks-list.html.

23 Emily Holden, 'Trump to Roll Back Obama-Era Clean Car Rules in Huge Blow to Climate Fight'. *The Guardian*, 31 March 2020. https://www.theguardian.com/environment/2020/mar/31/trump-epa-obama-clean-car-rules-climate-change.

24 Gaby Del Valle, 'When Environmentalism Meets Xenophobia'. *The Nation*, 8 November 2018. https://www.thenation.com/article/archive/environment-climate-eugenics-immigration/.

25 Celine Castronuovo, 'Tucker Carlson: Climate Change Is "Systemic Racism in the Sky"'. The Hill, 12 September 2020. https://thehill.com/homenews/media/516150-tucker-carl son-climate-change-is-systematic-racism-in-the-sky.

26 Alex Hochuli, 'The Brazilianization of the World', *American Affairs Journal* V, no. 2 (2021).

27 Philip Fearnside, 'Why Brazil's New President Poses an Unprecedented Threat to the Amazon'. Yale Environment 360, 8 November 2018. https://e360.yale.edu/features/why-brazils-new-president-poses-an-unprecedented-threat-to-the-amazon.

28 WWF Brazil, 'Deforestation in the Amazon Increased 30% between August 2018 and July 2019'. WWF, 18 November 2019. https://www.wwf.org.br/?74083/Deforestation-in-the-Amazon-increased-30-between-August-2018-and-July-2019.

29 Jake Spring and Lisandra Paraguassu, 'Deforestation in Brazil's Amazon Skyrockets to 12-Year High under Bolsonaro'. *Reuters*, 1 December 2020. https://www.reuters.com/article/brazil-environment-idUSKBN28B3MV.

30 Bruce Stokes, Richard Wike and Jill Carle, 'Global Concern about Climate Change, Broad Support for Limiting Emissions'. Pew Research Centre, 5 November 2015.

31 Fábio de Castro, 'Environmental Policies in the Lula Era: Accomplishments and Contradictions'. In Fábio de Castro, Kees Koonings and Marianne Wiesebron (eds.), *Brazil Under the Workers' Party: Continuity and Change from Lula to Dilma* (London: Palgrave Macmillan, 2014), 229–55, p. 231.

32 Brown, *In the Ruins of Neoliberalism*.

33 Glenn Greenwald and Victor Pougy, 'Exclusive: Brazil's Top Prosecutors Who Indicted Lula Schemed in Secret Messages to Prevent His Party From Winning 2018 Election'. The Intercept, 9 June 2019. https://theinter cept.com/2019/06/09/brazil-car-wash-prosecutors-workers-party-lula/.

34 Luisa Maria Diele-Viegas and Carlos Frederico Duarte

Rocha, 'Why Releasing Mining on Amazonian Indigenous Lands and the Advance of Agrobusiness Is Extremely Harmful for the Mitigation of World's Climate Change? Comment on Pereira et al. (Environmental Science & Policy 100 (2019) 8–12)'. *Environmental Science & Policy* 103, no. 2 (2020): 30–1.

35 Ana Guggenheim Coutinho, 'Politics of Devastation: Remarks on De-Democratization, Indigenous Peoples, and the Environment in Contemporary Brazil'. In Bernardo Bianchi, Jorge Chaloub, Patricia Rangel and Frieder Otto Wolf (eds.), *Democracy and Brazil: Collapse and Regression* (London: Routledge, 2020), p. 203.

36 Ibid., p. 196.

37 Jon Lee Anderson, 'At the U.N., Jair Bolsonaro Presents a Surreal Defense of His Amazon Policies'. *The New Yorker*, 25 September 2019.

38 Terrence McCoy, 'The Amazon Is Burning. Bolsonaro Says His Critics Are Setting the Fires, to Make Him Look Bad'. *The Washington Post*, 22 August 2019.

39 Tommy Beer, 'Majority of Republicans Believe the QAnon Conspiracy Theory Is Partly Or Mostly True, Survey Finds'. Forbes, 2 September 2020. https://www.forbes.com/sites/tommybeer/2020/09/02/majority-of-republicans-believe-the-qanon-conspiracy-theory-is-partly-or-mostly-true-survey-finds/.

40 Malm and the Zetkin Collective, *White Skin, Black Fuel*, pp. 20–1.

41 UN Environment Programme, 'Mitigation'. UNEP – UN Environment Programme, 14 September 2017. http://www.unenvironment.org/explore-topics/climate-change/what-we-do/mitigation; UNFCCC, 'What Do Adaptation to Climate Change and Climate Resilience Mean?' United Nations Climate Change. https://unfccc.int/topics/adaptation-and-resilience/the-big-picture/what-do-adaptation-to-climate-change-and-climate-resilience-mean.

42 Christian Parenti, *Tropic of Chaos: Climate Change and the New Geography of Violence* (New York: Nation Books, 2011), p. 18.

43 Bruno Latour, *Down to Earth: Politics in the New Climatic Regime* (Cambridge: Polity, 2018).

44 Michael Stothard, 'Marine Le Pen Uses Environmental

Issue to Broaden Appeal'. *Financial Times*, 26 January 2017.

45 Malm and the Zetkin Collective, *White Skin, Black Fuel*, p. 134.

46 Aude Mazoue, 'Le Pen's National Rally Goes Green in Bid for European Election Votes'. France 24, 20 April 2019. https://www.france24.com/en/20190420-le-pen-national-rally-front-environment-european-elections-france

47 Eirini Tountasaki, and Salomi Boukala, 'From Black to Green: Analysing Le Front National's "Patriotic Ecology"'. In Bernhard Forchtner (ed.), *The Far Right and the Environment* (Abingdon: Routledge, 2019), 72–87.

48 Stella Schaller and Alexander Carius, 'Convenient Truths: Mapping Climate Agendas of Right-Wing Populist Parties in Europe'. Adelphi, 26 February 2019, p. 83.

49 Hilary Moore, 'Burning Earth, Changing Europe: How the Racist Right Exploits Climate Crisis – and What We Can Do About It'. Rosa-Luxemburg-Stiftung, 6 March 2020. https://www.rosalux.eu/en/article/1588.burning-earth-changing-europe.html, p. 56.

50 Lise Benoist, 'Green Is the New Brown: Ecology in the Metapolitics of the Far Right'. Undisciplined Environments, 4 May 2021. https://undisciplinedenvironments.org/2021/05/04/green-is-the-new-brown-ecology-in-the-metapolitics-of-the-far-right/.

51 Schaller and Carius, 'Convenient Truths', p. 87.

52 Moore, 'Burning Earth, Changing Europe', p. 39.

53 Malm and the Zetkin Collective, *White Skin, Black Fuel*, pp. 90–3.

54 Ed King, 'Duterte: Addressing Climate Change Is "Top Priority" for Philippines'. Climate Home News, 25 July 2016. https://www.climatechangenews.com/2016/07/25/duterte-addressing-climate-change-is-top-priority-for-philippines/.

55 Al Jazeera, '"More Dangerous Every Day": Land Rights Defenders Killings Surge'. Al Jazeera, 29 July 2020. https://www.aljazeera.com/news/2020/7/29/more-dangerous-every-day-land-rights-defenders-killings-surge.

56 Muhammad Arfan, Jewell Lund, Daniyal Hassan, Maaz Saleem and Aftab Ahmad. 'Assessment of Spatial and Temporal Flow Variability of the Indus River'. *Resources* 8, no. 2 (2019): 103.

57 Eamonn Murphy, '"We Have No Orders to Save You":
    State Terrorism, Politics and Communal Violence in
    the Indian State of Gujarat, 2002'. In Richard Jackson,
    Eamonn Murphy, and Scott Poynting (eds.), *Contemporary
    State Terrorism: Theory and Practice* (London: Routledge,
    2011), 86–103.
58 Angana P. Chatterji, Thomas Blom Hansen and Christophe
    Jaffrelot, 'Introduction', in Christophe Jaffrelot, Thomas
    Blom Hansen and Angana P. Chatterji (eds.), *Majoritarian
    State* (New York: Oxford University Press, 2019), 1–18,
    pp. 3–4.
59 R.B. Moore, 'India's Hindu Nationalist Project Relies
    on Brutal Repression'. *Jacobin*, 16 April 2021. https://
    jacobinmag.com/2021/04/india-hindutva-nationalism-modi-
    repression.
60 Ibid.
61 Christophe Jaffrelot, 'A *De Facto* Ethnic Democracy?
    Obliterating and Targeting the Other, Hindu Vigilantes,
    and the Ethno-State'. In Christophe Jaffrelot, Thomas Blom
    Hansen, and Angana P. Chatterji (eds.), *Majoritarian State*
    (New York: Oxford University Press, 2019), 41–67.
62 Narendra Modi, *Convenient Action: Gujarat's Response
    to Challenges of Climate Change* (New Delhi: Macmillan
    Publishers India, 2011).
63 Jyoti Puri, 'Sculpting the Saffron Body: Yoga, Hindutva,
    and the International Marketplace'. In Christophe Jaffrelot,
    Thomas Blom Hansen, and Angana P. Chatterji (eds.),
    Majoritarian State (Oxford: Oxford University Press,
    2019), 317–32, pp. 326–7.
64 Puri, 'Sculpting the Saffron Body', p. 328.
65 IndiaToday, 'Teachers Day Speech: PM Modi Says No
    Climate Change', *India Today*, 14 September 2015. https://
    www.indiatoday.in/india/north/story/teachers-day-speech-
    pm-modi-says-no-climate-change-207413-2014-09-05.
66 Pune Mirror, 'The Floods Have Nothing to Do with
    Climate Change, Says Prakash Javadekar'. *Pune Mirror*,
    11 August 2019. https://punemirror.indiatimes.com/pune/
    others/the-floods-have-nothing-to-do-with-climate-change-
    says-prakash-javadekar/articleshow/70623764.cms.
67 Jacob Koshy, '99.82% Projects in Forests Got Nod'.
    The Hindu, 13 February 2019. https://www.thehindu.

com/news/national/9982-projects-in-forests-got-nod/arti
cle26261368.ece.

68 Sehaj Singh Cheema and Smita Gupta, 'How India's Draft
Environmental Impact Assessment Notification Impacts
Environmental Rights'. *Oxford Human Rights Hub*, 30
June 2020. https://web.archive.org/web/20201218035817/
https://ohrh.law.ox.ac.uk/how-indias-draft-environmen
tal-impact-assessment-notification-impacts-environmen
tal-rights/.

69 Kumar Sambhav Shrivastava, 'India Allows 16 New
Thermal Power Plants That Violate Stricter Air Pollution
Standards to Come Up', Scroll.in, 2 October 2017. https://
scroll.in/article/852288/india-allows-16-new-thermal-
power-plants-that-violate-stricter-air-pollution-standards-
to-come-up.

70 Praful Bidwai, 'Modi Government Cracks down on Green
NGOs'. openDemocracy, 17 February 2015. https://www.
opendemocracy.net/en/openglobalrights-openpage/modi-
government-cracks-down-on-green-ngos/.

71 Naomi Klein, 'India Targets Climate Activists with the
Help of Big Tech'. The Intercept, 27 February 2021. https://
theintercept.com/2021/02/27/india-climate-activists-twit
ter-google-facebook/.

72 Swansy Afonso, Rajesh Kumar Singh and Debjit
Chakraborty, 'Modi Overhaul of Green Rules Sparks Fears
of Return to Grim Past'. BloombergQuint, 9 September
2020. https://www.bloombergquint.com/business/modi-ov
erhaul-of-green-rules-sparks-fears-of-return-to-grim-past.

73 Ishan Kukreti, 'Char Dham National Highway Has Cost
Uttarakhand Its Ecological Balance'. DownToEarth,
3 January 2019. https://www.downtoearth.org.in/news/
environment/char-dham-national-highway-has-cost-utta
rakhand-its-ecological-balance-62661.

74 Moore, 'India's Hindu Nationalist Project'.

75 Varun Sivaram and Annushka Shivnani, 'India Warms
Up to Climate Action'. Council on Foreign Relations,
19 November 2015. https://www.cfr.org/expert-brief/
india-warms-climate-action.

76 Narendra Modi, 'PM's Address at "Samvad": Global Hindu-
Buddhist Initiative on Conflict Avoidance and Environment
Consciousness'. www.narendramodi.in, 3 September 2015.

https://www.narendramodi.in/text-of-pm-s-address-at-sam vad-global-hindu-buddhist-initiative-on-conflict-avoidance-and-environment-consciousness-290614.

77 Climate News Network. 'India Has an (Official) Climate Change of Heart'. *Climate News Network*, 23 December 2020. https://climatenewsnetwork.net/india-has-an-official-climate-change-of-heart/.

78 Suparna Chaudhry, 'India's New Law May Leave Millions of Muslims without Citizenship'. *The Washington Post*, 13 December 2019.

79 Aranyo Aarjan, 'Bengal Is Being Hit Hard by Climate Catastrophe'. Verso, 17 September 2020. https://www.versobooks.com/blogs/4856-hunger-or-the-social-logic-of-climate-breakdown.

80 Jordan Dyett and Cassidy Thomas, 'Overpopulation Discourse: Patriarchy, Racism, and the Specter of Ecofascism'. *Perspectives on Global Development and Technology* 18, no. 1–2 (2019): 205–24.

81 Hay, *Main Currents*.

82 Ibid., p. 187; Brown, *In the Ruins of Neoliberalism*.

83 Jørgen Randers, 'Demokratin har svårt att hantera klimathotet'. *Tidningen Extrakt*, 15 January 2015. https://www.extrakt.se/demokratin-oformogen-att-hantera-klimat hotet/.

84 David Shearman, 'Democracy and Climate Change: A Story of Failure'. openDemocracy, 7 November 2007. https://www.opendemocracy.net/en/democracy_and_clim ate_change_a_story_of_failure/.

85 David Shearman and Joseph Wayne Smith, *The Climate Change Challenge and the Failure of Democracy* (Westport, CT: Greenwood Press, 2007).

86 Daniel Fiorino, 'Improving Democracy for the Future: Why Democracy Can Handle Climate Change'. *E-International Relations*, 24 June 2019; Hay, *Main Currents*, p. 189.

87 Hay, *Main Currents*, pp. 188–9.

88 David W. Orr and Stuart Hill, 'Leviathan, the Open Society, and the Crisis of Ecology', *The Western Political Quarterly* 31, no. 4 (1978): 457–69, p. 464.

89 Matthew N. Lyons, 'Threat or Model?: US Rightists Look at China', *Three Way Fight*, 20 April 2020. http://three wayfight.blogspot.com/2020/04/threat-or-model-us-right

ists-look-at.html. See also Mark Beeson, 'The Coming of Environmental Authoritarianism'. *Environmental Politics* 19, no. 2 (2010): 276–94.

90 Yifei Li and Judith Shapiro, *China Goes Green: Coercive Environmentalism for a Troubled Planet* (Cambridge: Polity, 2020), p. 6.

91 Matt McGrath, 'Climate Change: China Aims for "Carbon Neutrality by 2060"'. BBC News, 22 September 2020. https://www.bbc.com/news/science-environment-54256826.

92 Li and Shapiro, *China Goes Green*, p. 6.

93 Ibid., p. 23.

94 Ibid., p. 50–5.

95 Ibid., p. 55–7.

96 Teresa Wright, *Popular Protest in China* (Cambridge: Polity, 2018), pp. 135–6.

97 Sabrina Habich, *Dams, Migration and Authoritarianism: The Local State in Yunnan* (New York: Routledge, 2018), pp. 49–51.

98 Dokku Nagamalleswara Rao and Atmaja Gohain Baruah, 'Is China Going Green by Dumping Brown on Its BRI Partners?', East Asia Forum, 25 September 2018. https://www.eastasiaforum.org/2018/09/25/is-china-going-green-by-dumping-brown-on-its-bri-partners/.

99 Brian La Shier, 'Exploring the Environmental Repercussions of China's Belt and Road Initiative', EESI, 30 October 2018, https://www.eesi.org/articles/view/exploring-the-environmental-repercussions-of-chinas-belt-and-road-initiativ; Fernando Ascensão, Lenore Fahrig, Anthony P. Clevenger, et al., 'Environmental Challenges for the Belt and Road Initiative', *Nature Sustainability* 1, no. 5 (2018): 206–9.

100 Xiaoying You, Jianqiang Liu and Hongqiao Liu, 'Q&A: What Does China's 14th "Five Year Plan" Mean for Climate Change?' Carbon Brief, 12 March 2021. https://www.carbonbrief.org/qa-what-does-chinas-14th-five-year-plan-mean-for-climate-change.

101 Nicholas Stern and Chunping Xie, 'China's New Growth Story'. London: Grantham Research Institute on Climate Change and the Environment, March 2021.

102 Marina Povitkina, 'The Limits of Democracy in Tackling Climate Change'. *Environmental Politics* 27, no. 3 (2018): 411–32.

103 Brown, *In the Ruins of Neoliberalism*.
104 John S. Dryzek and Simon Niemeyer, 'Deliberative Democracy and Climate Governance'. *Nature Human Behaviour* 3, no. 5 (2019): 411–13.
105 Rajiv Ghimire, Nathaniel Anbar and Netra B. Chhetri, 'The Impact of Public Deliberation on Climate Change Opinions Among U.S. Citizens'. *Frontiers in Political Science* 3 (2021).
106 Climate Home News, 'French Draft Climate Law Criticised for Weakening Ambition of Citizens' Assembly'. Climate Home News, 12 January 2021. https://www.climatechangenews. com/2021/01/12/french-draft-climate-law-criticised-weak ening-ambition-citizens-assembly/.

Chapter 3: Online far-right ecologism and far-right movements

1 Anonymous, 'Where the Fuck Did Everyone Go?' *8kun*, 31 August 2020. http://archive.is/ali1G.
2 For a much fuller account, see 'Influencer and Swarm', in Moore and Roberts, *Post-Internet Far Right*.
3 Jennifer Kent, 'Individualized Responsibility: "If Climate Protection Becomes Everyone's Responsibility, Does It End up Being No-One's?"' *Cosmopolitan Civil Societies: An Interdisciplinary Journal* 1, no. 3 (2009): 132–49.
4 See, for example, Hope Not Hate, 'More Links Between Generation Identity and Christchurch Mosque Killer Emerge', 15 May 2019. https://www.hopenothate.org.uk/ 2019/05/15/more-links-between-generation-identity-and-christchurch-mosque-killer-emerge/.
5 Richard Spencer, 'What It Means To Be Alt-Right'. Alt-Right, 11 August 2017. https://altright.com/2017/08/11/ what-it-means-to-be-alt-right/.
6 Pietro Castelli Gattinara and Catarina Froio, 'CasaPound Italia: Contemporary Extreme Right Politics', 27 April 2020. https://www.sv.uio.no/c-rex/english/news-and-events/ right-now/2020/2020-03-casapound-italia-contemporary-ex treme-right.html.
7 Erica X. Eisen, 'Italy's Green Fascists'. *Jewish Currents*, 18 September 2019. https://jewishcurrents.org/italys-green-fas cists/.

8 Arthur Versluis, 'A Conversation About Radicalism in Contemporary Greece'. *Journal for the Study of Radicalism* 10, no. 1 (2016): 145–62, pp. 159–60.
9 Golden Dawn Newsroom, 'The Green Wing and the Volksland Project'. Golden Dawn – International Newsroom, n.d.   http://golden-dawn-international-newsroom.blogspot. com/p/the-green-wing-and-volksland.html.
10 Schaller and Carius. 'Convenient Truths', p. 86.
11 Golden Dawn Newsroom. 'The Green Wing'.
12 On the resistance of actual blood to its mythic appropriation, see Grove, *Savage Ecology*, ch. 5.
13 CasaPound, 'La Foresta che Avanza'. CasaPound Italia, 27 July 2020. https://www.casapounditalia.org/la-foresta-che-avanza/.
14 The National Justice Party, 'The Platform of The National Justice Party'. The National Justice Party, November 2020. https://nationaljusticeparty.com/platform/.
15 Warren Balogh, 'A Message to the Left'. 19 November 2020. https://nationaljusticeparty.com/2020/11/19/a-message-to-the-left/.
16 Laura Towler, 'Indigenous Peoples Day 2020'. Patriotic Alternative, 9 August 2020. https://www.patrioticalterna tive.org.uk/indigenous_peoples_day_2020.
17 Padraig Kirwan and David Stirrup, '"I'm Indiginous, I'm Indiginous, I'm Indiginous": Indigenous Rights, British Nationalism, and the European Far Right'. In James Mackay and David Stirrup (ed.), *Tribal Fantasies: Native Americans in the European Imaginary, 1900–2010* (New York: Palgrave Macmillan, 2013), 59–83.
18 Ibid., p. 67.
19 Elizabeth Schumacher, 'German Right-Wing AfD Party Fears Radicalization of Youth Wing'. DW.COM, 26 November 2018. https://www.dw.com/en/german-right-wing-afd-party-fears-radicalization-of-youth-wing/a-46449323.
20 Kaja Zimmermann, 'How the German Right Reacts to Youth Climate Activism'. *Green European Journal*, 28 July 2020.   https://www.greeneuropeanjournal.eu/how-the-ger man-right-reacts-to-youth-climate-activism/.
21 Joseph Nasr, 'Save Coal, Lose Youth Vote? Far-Right German Party Faces Climate Policy Revolt'. *Reuters*, 30 May

2019. https://www.reuters.com/article/us-germany-afd-idUS KCN1SZ1KD.

22 Mike Ma, *Harassment Architecture* (independently published, 2019), p. 40.

23 Ibid., p. 22.

24 Makuch, 'Fascists Impersonate Climate Group'.

25 Simon Childs, 'Local Green Group Actually a Front for Far-Right Activists'. VICE, 27 November 2020. https://www.vice.com/en/article/93wkk7/generation-identity-uk-local-matters-far-right.

26 Neal Spencer and Brahmin, 'The McSpencer Group – September 19, 2019'. https://player.fm/series/the-spencer-report-2739326/the-mcspencer-group-september-19-2019, 43:00–43:30, 53:00–53:44.

27 Ibid., 50:44–51:35.

28 Bronze Age Pervert, *Bronze Age Mindset* (independently published, 2018), Prologue.

29 Ibid., section 68.

30 P.W. Singer, *Corporate Warriors: The Rise of the Privatized Military Industry* (Ithaca, NY: Cornell University Press, 2008), p. 37.

31 Bronze Age Pervert, *Bronze Age Mindset*, section 63.

32 Ibid., section 78.

33 Ben Schreckinger, 'The Alt-Right Manifesto That Has Trumpworld Talking'. POLITICO, 23 August 2019. https://politi.co/2zisMUA.

34 Karim Zidan, 'North Pack: British MMA Fight Club "Heritage and Culture" Forced to Shut Down'. Bloody Elbow, 24 September 2019. https://www.bloodyelbow.com/2019/9/24/20879934/british-mma-fight-club-promoting-heritage-culture-shut-down-backlash-alt-right-neo-nazi-politics.

35 The language of tributaries is not intended to suggest that everything in these cultures has fed into the far right, or that these cultures have been subsumed by the far right.

36 Seth Brown, 'Alex Jones's Infowars Media Empire Is Built to Sell Snake-Oil Diet Supplements'. Intelligencer, 4 May 2017. https://nymag.com/intelligencer/2017/05/how-does-alex-jones-make-money.html.

37 Moore, *Capitalism*.

38 Moore and Roberts, *Post-Internet Far Right*, ch. 3.
39 Klaus Theweleit, *Male Fantasies Volume 1: Women, Floods, Bodies, History* (Minneapolis, MN: University of Minnesota Press, 1987).
40 Ma, *Harassment Architecture*, pp. 150–1.
41 Amy Harmon, 'Why White Supremacists Are Chugging Milk (and Why Geneticists Are Alarmed)'. *The New York Times*, 17 October 2018. https://www.nytimes.com/2018/10/17/us/white-supremacists-science-dna.html.
42 See Paul B. Preciado, *Testo Junkie: Sex, Drugs and Biopolitics in the Pharmacopornographic Era* (New York: The Feminist Press, 2013).
43 Spandrell, 'Biological Leninism'. *Bloody Shovel 3*, 13 November 2017. https://spandrell.com/2017/11/14/biological-leninism/.
44 Bronze Age Pervert, *Bronze Age Mindset*, section 62.
45 Ward and Voas, 'Emergence of Conspirituality'.
46 Andrew Wilson, '#whitegenocide, the Alt-Right and Conspiracy Theory: How Secrecy and Suspicion Contributed to the Mainstreaming of Hate'. *Secrecy and Society* 1, no. 2 (2018), p. 10
47 Shannon Weber, 'White Supremacy's Old Gods'. Political Research Associates, 1 February 2018. https://www.politicalresearch.org/2018/02/01/white-supremacys-old-gods-the-far-right-and-neopaganism.
48 Nicholas Goodrick-Clarke, *Black Sun: Aryan Cults, Esoteric Nazism, and the Politics of Identity* (New York: New York University Press, 2002).
49 Christophe Bonneuil and Jean-Baptiste Fressoz, *The Shock of the Anthropocene: The Earth, History and Us* (London: Verso, 2017).
50 See Edward Dutton, Guy Madison and Curtis Dunkel, 'The Mutant Says in His Heart, "There Is No God": The Rejection of Collective Religiosity Centred Around the Worship of Moral Gods Is Associated with High Mutational Load'. *Evolutionary Psychological Science* 4, no. 3 (2018): 233–44.
51 Richard Spencer and Edward Dutton, 'The Religious Origins of the SJW'. The McSpencer Group. https://player.fm/series/the-spencer-report-2739326. See also Edward Dutton, 'The Next Great Awakening'. *Radix Journal* (blog), 27 June

2020. https://radixjournal.com/2020/06/the-next-great-awa kening/.

52 Beuret, 'Containing Climate Change', p. 5.

53 Ibid.

54 Andrew Ross, 'The Lonely Hour of Scarcity'. *Capitalism Nature Socialism* 7, no. 3 (1996): 3–26.

55 Jack Donovan, *The Way of Men* (Milwaukie, OR: Dissonant Hum, 2012), ch. 1.

56 Greenline Front International, '5 Differences between NS and Anti-Fascist Ecologism'. *Greenline Front International* (blog), July 2016. http://greenlinefront.blogspot.com/2016/07/5-differences-between-ns-and-anti.html.

57 Alexandra Stern, *Proud Boys and the White Ethnostate: How the Alt-Right Is Warping the American Imagination* (Boston, MA: Beacon Press, 2019), ch. 2.

58 Ben Etherington, 'The New Primitives'. *Los Angeles Review of Books*, 24 May 2018. https://lareviewofbooks.org/article/the-new-primitives/.

59 Ibid.

60 Brown, *In the Ruins of Neoliberalism*; Moore and Roberts, *Post-Internet Far Right*, ch. 1.

Chapter 4: Deadly ecofascist violence

1 Sindre Bangstad, 'Bat Ye'or and Eurabia'. In Mark J. Sedgwick (ed.), *Key Thinkers of the Radical Right: Behind the New Threat to Liberal Democracy* (New York: Oxford University Press, 2019), 170–83.

2 Jennifer Wilson, 'White Flight: Nationalists Take on the Shifting Grounds of Polish Racial Identity'. *World Policy Journal* 35, no. 1 (2018): 26–9.

3 Greenline, '5 Differences between NS and Anti-Fascist Ecologism'.

4 Spandrell, 'Lee Kuan Yew Drains Your Brains for Short Term Gain'. *Bloody Shovel* (blog), 3 June 2015. https://web.archive.org/web/20150603222710/https://bloodyshovel.wordpress.com/2013/03/26/lee-kuan-yew-drains-your-brains-for-short-term-gain/; Nick Land, 'Modernity's Fertility Problem'. *Jacobite*, 20 June 2017. https://jacobitemag.com/2017/06/20/modernitys-fertility-problem/.

5 Roger Griffin, *Terrorist's Creed: Fanatical Violence and the Human Need for Meaning* (Basingstoke: Palgrave, 2012), p. 15.
6 Stern, *Proud Boys*.
7 Northwest Front, 'The NF Program', n.d. http://north westfront.org/about/northwest-front-program/ (no longer available).
8 Greg Johnson, 'Restoring White Homelands'. Counter-Currents, 24 June 2014. https://counter-currents.com/2014/06/the-slow-cleanse/.
9 Rinaldo Nazzaro, Blake, and Kiz. *The Base*. Blake and Kiz Power Hour. https://www.bitchute.com/video/5vfY7If7dY8w/.
10 Ibid., 1:16:54–1:17:13
11 Zachary Kamel, Mack Lamoureux and Ben Makuch, '"Eco-Fascist" Arm of Neo-Nazi Terror Group, The Base, Linked to Swedish Arson'. VICE News, 29 January 2020. https://www.vice.com/en/article/qjdvzx/eco-fascist-arm-of-neo-nazi-terror-group-the-base-linked-to-swedish-arson.
12 Nazzaro et al., *The Base*, 1:38:10–1:39:39
13 Rinaldo Nazzaro, *Guerrilla Warfare Theory by Rinaldo Nazzaro – The Definitive Compilation (2018)*, 2019. https://web.archive.org/web/20190916153722/https://www.bitchute.com/video/x6QJMXBTQ0eE/, 29:13.
14 Knute Berger, 'Hate-Filled Zone: The Racist Roots of a Northwest Secession Movement'. Crosscut, 8 July 2015. https://crosscut.com/2015/07/hate-filled-zone-a-group-of-white-racists-wants-a-nw-secession-a-vile-dream-with-deep-historic-roots.
15 Ben Makuch and Mack Lamoureux, 'Neo-Nazi Terror Leader Said to Have Worked with US Special Forces'. VICE News, 24 September 2020. https://www.vice.com/en/article/k7qdzv/neo-nazi-terror-leader-said-to-have-worked-with-us-special-forces.
16 Jason Wilson, 'Revealed: The True Identity of the Leader of an American Neo-Nazi Terror Group'. *The Guardian*, 24 January 2020. https://www.theguardian.com/world/2020/jan/23/revealed-the-true-identity-of-the-leader-of-americas-neo-nazi-terror-group.
17 Ibid.
18 Tony Odarg, 'Duginism in Action: Paramilitary "the

Base" Founder Rinaldo Nazzaro Is a Russian Intelligence Contractor'. 19 February 2020. https://web.archive.org/web/20210218183525/https://www.bitchute.com/video/JQfAwkIrnCj8/.

19 Bill Chappell, Merrit Kennedy and Vanessa Romo, '3 Alleged Members of Hate Group "The Base" Arrested in Georgia, Another in Wisconsin'. NPR, 17 January 2020. https://www.npr.org/2020/01/17/797399834/3-alleged-mem bers-of-hate-group-the-base-arrested-in-georgia.

20 On the post-Vietnam wave, see Belew, *Bring the War Home*.

21 Patrik Hermansson and David Lawrence, 'Hitler Youths: The Rise of Teenage Far-Right Terrorists'. HOPE not Hate, September 2020, p. 15.

22 Austmador, 'Fascism Is Nature'. *Eco Fascist Order*, 19 October 2018. https://web.archive.org/web/20181116184129/https://ecofascistorder.wordpress.com/2018/10/19/fascism-is-nat ure/.

23 Tim Turtle, 'Animal Welfare'. *The American Futurist*, 10 November 2020. https://www.americanfuturist.xyz/2020/11/10/animal-welfare/.

24 Daniel Friberg, 'The Metapolitical Vanguard of the Right', in *The Real Right Returns* (London: Arktos Media, 2015), p. 25.

25 Moore and Roberts, *Post-Internet Far Right*, ch. 8.

26 Forchtner, 'Eco-Fascism'.

Chapter 5: Towards ecofascism proper?

1 Max Horkheimer and Theodor W. Adorno, *Dialectic of Enlightenment: Philosophical Fragments*, ed. by Gunzelin Schmid Noerr, trans. by Edmund Jephcott (Stanford, CA: Stanford University Press, 2002), p. 173.

2 Stuart Hall, *The Hard Road to Renewal: Thatcherism and the Crisis of the Left* (London: Verso, 1988), p. 34.

3 Eric Bonds, 'Upending Climate Violence Research: Fossil Fuel Corporations and the Structural Violence of Climate Change'. *Human Ecology Review* 22, no. 2 (2016): 3–23.

4 Malm and the Zetkin Collective, *White Skin, Black Fuel*.

5 Parenti, 'Hard State versus Failed State', in *Tropic of Chaos*.

6 Geoff Eley, 'Broadside for the Trump Era: Is Trump a

Fascist?', Verso, 19 March 2018, https://www.versobooks. com/blogs/3697-broadside-for-the-trump-era-is-trump-a-fascist.

7 Dorceta E. Taylor, *The Rise of the American Conservation Movement: Power, Privilege, and Environmental Protection* (Durham, NC: Duke University Press, 2016), p. 21.

8 The term 'New Cold War' is highly contentious. We use it here to reflect its likely future presentation in far-right politics, not because we think the comparison is warranted.

9 Devin Zane Shaw, 'Between System-Loyal Vigilantism and System-Oppositional Violence'. *Three Way Fight* (blog), 25 October 2020. http://threewayfight.blogspot.com/2020/10/between-system-loyal-vigilantism-and.html.

10 Jaspar Bernes, 'Between the Devil and the Green New Deal'. *Commune*, 25 April 2019. https://communemag.com/between-the-devil-and-the-green-new-deal/.

11 Martín Arboleda, *Planetary Mine: Territories of Extraction under Late Capitalism* (Brooklyn, NY: Verso Books, 2020).

12 Matt Mandel, 'Experts: Shale Revolution Has Improved US Energy Security and Is "Shifting the Geopolitical Balance"'. *Energy In Depth*, 25 May 2018. https://www.energyindepth. org/experts-shale-revolution-improved-u-s-energy-security-shifting-geopolitical-balance/.

13 Malm, *How to Blow up a Pipeline*, pp. 54–6.

14 Parenti, 'Hard State versus Failed State', in *Tropic of Chaos*.

15 Sujatha Raman, 'Fossilizing Renewable Energies'. *Science as Culture* 22, no. 2 (2013): 172–80.

16 Arboleda, *Planetary Mine*.

17 Lyons, 'Threat or Model?'.

18 Bernes, 'Between the Devil and the Green New Deal'; see also Helen Thompson, 'The Geopolitical Fight to Come over Green Energy'. *Engelsberg Ideas*, 5 March 2021. https://engelsbergideas.com/essays/the-geopolitical-fight-to-come-over-green-energy/.

19 Glenn Greenwald and Evo Morales, 'Watch: Glenn Greenwald's Exclusive Interview with Bolivia's Evo Morales, Who Was Deposed in a Coup'. The Intercept, 16 December 2019; Kinga Harasim, 'Bolivia's Lithium Coup'. *Latin America Bureau*, 8 December 2020; Kate Aronoff, 'The Socialist Win in Bolivia and the New Era

of Lithium Extraction'. *The New Republic*, 19 October 2020. For the opposing view, see Keith Johnson and James Palmer, 'Bolivia's Lithium Isn't the New Oil'. *Foreign Policy*, 13 November 2019.

20 Matthew Rozsa, 'Elon Musk Becomes Twitter Laughingstock after Bolivian Socialist Movement Returns to Power'. Salon, 20 October 2020. https://www.salon.com/2020/10/20/ elon-musk-becomes-twitter-laughingstock-after-bolivian-so cialist-movement-returns-to-power/.

21 Jorge Antonio Rocha, 'Bolivia Hints Tesla's Involvement in 2019 Military Coup'. Anadolu Agency, 24 March 2021. https://www.aa.com.tr/en/americas/bolivia-hints-teslas-in volvement-in-2019-military-coup/2187164.

22 Yannick Fischer, 'Basic Income, Labour Automation and Migration – An Approach from a Republican Perspective'. *Basic Income Studies* 15, no. 2 (2020).

23 Malm and the Zetkin Collective, *White Skin, Black Fuel*, pp. 162–4.

24 Manuel R. Torres-Soriano and Mario Toboso-Buezo, 'Five Terrorist Dystopias'. *The International Journal of Intelligence, Security, and Public Affairs* 21, no. 1 (2019): 49–65.

25 Sean Fleming, 'The Unabomber and the Origins of Anti-Tech Radicalism'. *Journal of Political Ideologies*, https://doi. org/10.1080/13569317.2021.1921940, 1–19.

26 Torres-Soriano and Toboso-Buezo, 'Five Terrorist Dystopias'.

27 Parenti, *Tropic of Chaos*.

28 For a different take on this same totalizing process, see Mann and Wainwright, *Climate Leviathan*. The central difference here is that we see the control that each of our futures represents as precisely depending on the global fragmentation of forms of governance.

29 Mann, *Fascists*, p. 2.

30 Naomi Klein, *The Shock Doctrine: The Rise of Disaster Capitalism* (London: Penguin, 2008); Antony Loewenstein, *Disaster Capitalism: Making a Killing out of Catastrophe* (London: Verso Books, 2015).

31 Beuret, 'Containing Climate Change', p. 7.

32 Ibid.

33 Ibid., p. 8.

34 Andrew E. Kramer, 'Russia, Crippled by Drought, Bans Grain Exports'. *The New York Times*, 5 August 2010, sec. World. https://www.nytimes.com/2010/08/06/world/europe/06russia.html. Andrew E. Kramer, 'Drought in Russia Ripples Beyond the Wheat Fields'. *The New York Times*, 27 August 2010, sec. Business. https://www.nytimes.com/2010/08/28/business/global/28wheat.html.

35 All this has been disputed. See, for example, Jan Selby, Omar S. Dahi, Christiane Fröhlich and Mike Hulme, 'Climate Change and the Syrian Civil War Revisited'. *Political Geography* 60 (2017): 232–44.

36 Neil Davidson and Richard Saull, 'Neoliberalism and the Far-Right: A Contradictory Embrace'. *Critical Sociology* 43, no. 4–5 (2017): 707–24.

37 Joshua Clover, 'The Rise and Fall of Biopolitics: A Response to Bruno Latour'. *In the Moment* (blog), 29 March 2020. https://critinq.wordpress.com/2020/03/29/the-rise-and-fall-of-biopolitics-a-response-to-bruno-latour/.

38 Jakub Wondreys and Cas Mudde, 'Victims of the Pandemic? European Far-Right Parties and COVID-19'. *Nationalities Papers*, 21 October 2020, 1–18.

39 Sebastian Doerr, Stefan Gissler, José-Luis Peydró and Hans-Joachim Voth, 'From Finance to Fascism', 3 November 2020. http://dx.doi.org/10.2139/ssrn.3146746.

40 Francesco Lamperti, Valentina Bosetti, Andrea Roventini and Massimo Tavoni, 'The Public Costs of Climate-Induced Financial Instability'. *Nature Climate Change* 9, no. 11 (2019): 829–33.

41 Aaron Benanav, 'Crisis and Recovery', *Phenomenal World*, 3 April 2020. https://phenomenalworld.org/analysis/crisis-and-recovery.

42 Dylan Riley, 'What Is Trump?' *New Left Review* 114 (2018).

43 Roman Vakulchuk, Indra Overland and Daniel Scholten, 'Renewable Energy and Geopolitics: A Review'. *Renewable and Sustainable Energy Reviews* 122 (2020): 109547.

44 Jairus Grove, 'War and Militarization'. In Mark Juergensmeyer, Saskia Sassen, Manfred B. Steger and Victor Faessel (eds.), *The Oxford Handbook of Global Studies* (Oxford: Oxford University Press, 2018), 382–98, p. 385.

45 Christopher Paul and Miriam Matthews, 'The Russian "Firehose of Falsehood" Propaganda Model'. RAND Corporation, 11 July 2016. https://www.rand.org/pubs/perspectives/PE198.html.

46 Samuel Forsythe and Anna Rößing, 'The War for the Future'. *New Perspectives* 28, no. 3 (2020): 330–46.

47 Belew, *Bring the War Home*.

48 Javier Jordan, 'Political and Social Trends in the Future of Global Security. A Meta-Study on Official Perspectives in Europe and North America'. *European Journal of Futures Research* 5, no. 1 (2017): 11; Katharina Nett and Lukas Rüttinger, 'Insurgency, Terrorism and Organised Crime in a Warming Climate'. Berlin: adelphi research gemeinnützige GmbH, October 2016, p. vi.

49 Parenti, *Tropic of Chaos*, p. 37.

50 Ibid.

51 Hayes, 'Colonising the Future', p. 47.

52 Bonds, 'Upending Climate Violence Research'.

53 Phillipe Le Billon, 'Resources, Wars and Violence'. In Raymond L. Bryant (ed.), *The International Handbook of Political Ecology* (Cheltenham: Edward Elgar Publishing, 2017).

54 William B. Gail, 'A New Dark Age Looms'. *The New York Times*, 19 April 2016. https://www.nytimes.com/2016/04/19/opinion/a-new-dark-age-looms.html.

55 James Bridle, 'The Future Will Be Bumpy'. Verso, 28 November 2019. https://www.versobooks.com/blogs/4507-the-future-will-be-bumpy.

56 Deborah R. Coen, *Climate in Motion: Science, Empire, and the Problem of Scale* (Chicago, IL: University of Chicago Press, 2018), p. 2.

57 Sörlin and Wormbs. 'Environing Technologies', p. 102.

58 Mann, *Fascists*, p. 13.

59 Riley, *The Civic Foundations*, Preface.

60 Amin, 'Return of Fascism'.

61 Mann, *Fascists*, p. 13.

62 Césaire, *Discourse on Colonialism*.

Conclusion

1 Parenti, *Tropic of Chaos*.
2 The argument is, in brief, that the Russian harvest failed because of climate change, leading to raised grain prices across the Middle East. It is, however, disputed. See Selby et al., 'Climate Change'.
3 The flip side – Scooby-Doo anti-fascism, in which the mask of any given political movement is removed to reveal fascism – is, of course, equally undesirable.
4 Isaac Stanley, Adrienne Buller and Matthew Lawrence, 'Caring for the Earth, Caring for Each Other: A Radical Industrial Strategy for Adult Social Care'. Common Wealth, October 2020.
5 Chris Saltmarsh, 'Green Socialism'. In Grace Blakeley (ed.), *Futures of Socialism: The General Election, the Pandemic and the Post-Corbyn Era* (Brooklyn, NY: Verso Books, 2020), p. 172.
6 Kurt Campbell, Jay Gulledge, J. McNeill, et al., *The Age of Consequences: The Foreign Policy and National Security Implications of Global Climate Change* (Washington, DC: Center for Strategic and International Studies and Center for a New American Security, 2007).
7 Herbert H. Haines, *Black Radicals and the Civil Rights Mainstream, 1954–1970* (Knoxville, TN: University of Tennessee Press, 1988).
8 For a similar argument, see Angela Williams, 'Solidarity, Justice and Climate Change Law'. *Melbourne Journal of International Law* 10, no. 2 (2009): 493–508.
9 This is roughly the distinction between the 'factual' and the 'normative' layers of solidarity made in Kurt Bayertz, 'Four Uses of "Solidarity"'. In Kurt Bayertz (ed.), *Solidarity* (Dordrecht: Springer Netherlands, 1999), 3–28, p. 3.
10 Jason Moore, 'The Capitalocene and Planetary Justice'. *Maize*, 11 July 2019.
11 Keston Sutherland, *Poetical Works 1999–2015* (London: Enitharmon Press, 2015), p. 355.
12 Beuret, 'Containing Climate Change', p. 20.
13 Moore, 'The Capitalocene and Planetary Justice'.

14 Shane Burley, 'Introduction: The Socialism of Fools'. *Journal of Social Justice* 9 (2019): 1–16, p. 4.

15 Parenti, 'Capitalism versus Nature?', in *Tropic of Chaos*.

16 Samir Gandesha (ed.), *Spectres of Fascism: Historical, Theoretical and International Perspectives* (London: Pluto Press, 2020).

17 Murray Bookchin, 'Utopia, Not Futurism: Why Doing the Impossible Is the Most Rational Thing We Can Do'. http://unevenearth.org/tag/environmentalism/.